Building Applications with Spring 5 and Kotlin

Build scalable and reactive applications with Spring, combined with the productivity of Kotlin

Miloš Vasić

BIRMINGHAM - MUMBAI

Building Applications with Spring 5 and Kotlin

Commissioning Editor: Aaron Lazar
Acquisition Editor: Sandeep Mishra
Content Development Editor: Zeeyan Pinheiro
Technical Editor: Ketan Kamble
Copy Editor: Safis Editing
Project Coordinator: Vaidehi Sawant
Proofreader: Safis Editing
Indexer: Rekha Nair
Graphics: Jason Monteiro
Production Coordinator: Shantanu Zagade

First published: May 2018

Production reference: 1170518

Published by Packt Publishing Ltd.
Livery Place
35 Livery Street
Birmingham
B3 2PB, UK.

ISBN 978-1-78839-480-2

www.packtpub.com

`mapt.io`

Mapt is an online digital library that gives you full access to over 5,000 books and videos, as well as industry leading tools to help you plan your personal development and advance your career. For more information, please visit our website.

Why subscribe?

- Spend less time learning and more time coding with practical eBooks and Videos from over 4,000 industry professionals

- Improve your learning with Skill Plans built especially for you

- Get a free eBook or video every month

- Mapt is fully searchable

- Copy and paste, print, and bookmark content

PacktPub.com

Did you know that Packt offers eBook versions of every book published, with PDF and ePub files available? You can upgrade to the eBook version at `www.PacktPub.com` and, as a print book customer, you are entitled to a discount on the eBook copy. Get in touch with us at `service@packtpub.com` for more details.

At `www.PacktPub.com`, you can also read a collection of free technical articles, sign up for a range of free newsletters, and receive exclusive discounts and offers on Packt books and eBooks.

Contributors

About the author

Miloš Vasić is a software engineer, author, and open source enthusiast. Miloš holds a bachelor's degree in the programming of computer graphics and a master's degree in the field of Android programming; he obtained both degrees at Singidunum University. He published his first book, *Fundamental Kotlin*, in October 2016 and thus achieved his dream of becoming an author. When he is not writing a new book, Miloš can be found working on his open source projects.

About the reviewers

Mario Arias is a software engineer and Spring certified instructor with more than 12 years of experience in software development and design, databases, training material design, and training delivery. He currently works as a software engineer in Manchester, UK, for Cake Solutions Ltd., a BAMTECH media company.

Mario is a well-known member of the Kotlin community and is part of the Arrow team, the group that developed and maintains the Arrow functional library. In his free time, he rides his bicycle and trains in Brazilian Jiu-Jitsu.

Nenad Đorđević has 22 years of experience in software development, engineering, and project and team management for software solutions developed in Java and JavaScript. He has been a part of international projects at U.S.Steel Kosice and U.S.Steel North America.

Nenad's expertise and career goals are focused on designing full-stack solutions using Java, Spring, and JavaScript modern frameworks.

Packt is searching for authors like you

If you're interested in becoming an author for Packt, please visit `authors.packtpub.com` and apply today. We have worked with thousands of developers and tech professionals, just like you, to help them share their insight with the global tech community. You can make a general application, apply for a specific hot topic that we are recruiting an author for, or submit your own idea.

Table of Contents

Preface

Spring is the most popular framework for web development and, every year, more and more developers are getting involved in Spring development. Spring Framework makes it possible to develop applications for the web, especially RESTful and other types of services. So far, all development has been undertaken in Java. Recently, Kotlin has become very popular! Due to this, and the huge growth of the Kotlin community, we decided to introduce you to Spring development by using Kotlin as the primary development programming language.

With Kotlin, you can do everything you could do with Java, but with more joy and fun! We will show you how to play with Spring and Kotlin and how to create amazing things! Take your seat and get ready for an amazing journey!

Who this book is for

This book is designed for people who would like to learn the Spring Framework, and who have a basic knowledge of Kotlin, but not of Spring. It's intended as a guide for newbie Spring programmers. In this book, all examples are given in pure Kotlin.

What this book covers

Chapter 1, *Starting Up*, starts preparing the working environment by setting up Git repositories. After we do that, we will use Gradle as a tool to shape our project and its modules.

Chapter 2, *Starting with Spring*, shows how to set up our development environment. We will be ready to create our first Spring code written in Kotlin.

Chapter 3, *Building Your First Spring RESTful Service with Kotlin*, defines the Spring project and lists examples along with tips on how to write nice and clean REST services with Spring using Kotlin.

Chapter 4, *Working with Spring Data JPA and MySQL*, describes Spring Data. We will see how to create a data repository with CRUD operations on some entity. Finally, we will learn how to make queries on the MySQL database.

Chapter 5, *Securing Applications with Spring Security*, presents Spring Security projects and shows some examples of how to utilize Basic Authentication and/or OAuth2.

Chapter 6, *Spring Cloud*, explains the difference between the microservice architecture and SOA. At the end, we will see how to use the Spring Cloud project to implement the microservice architecture in its own application.

Chapter 7, *Using Project Reactor*, discusses the advantages of reactive programming. We will present Project Reactor and teach the reader how to use its power in its applications.

Chapter 8, *Development Practices*, talks about some good and some not-so-good practices.

Chapter 9, *Testing*, explains the importance of well-tested code. We will see how to write JUnit tests with Kotlin and how to write tests for Spring-based applications.

Chapter 10, *Project Deployment*, finally, presents the different options for deploying Spring applications. We will also see how to deploy REST service to the Tomcat application server or to AWS. If you are a fan of AWS, this is a great topic for you!

To get the most out of this book

To get the most out of this book, read it slowly and carefully and do each of the examples we do. Try to understand the point behind the example given and how you would use it as a base to build something bigger. Also, as always, code as much as you can!

Download the example code files

You can download the example code files for this book from your account at www.packtpub.com. If you purchased this book elsewhere, you can visit www.packtpub.com/support and register to have the files emailed directly to you.

You can download the code files by following these steps:

1. Log in or register at www.packtpub.com.
2. Select the **SUPPORT** tab.
3. Click on **Code Downloads & Errata**.
4. Enter the name of the book in the **Search** box and follow the onscreen instructions.

Once the file is downloaded, please make sure that you unzip or extract the folder using the latest version of:

- WinRAR/7-Zip for Windows
- Zipeg/iZip/UnRarX for Mac
- 7-Zip/PeaZip for Linux

The code bundle for the book is also hosted on GitHub at `https://github.com/PacktPublishing/Building-Applications-with-Spring-5-and-Kotlin`. In case there's an update to the code, it will be updated on the existing GitHub repository.

We also have other code bundles from our rich catalog of books and videos available at `https://github.com/PacktPublishing/`. Check them out!

Download the color images

We also provide a PDF file that has color images of the screenshots/diagrams used in this book. You can download it here: `https://www.packtpub.com/sites/default/files/downloads/BuildingApplicationswithSpring5andKotlin_ColorImages.pdf`.

Conventions used

There are a number of text conventions used throughout this book.

`CodeInText`: Indicates code words in text, database table names, folder names, filenames, file extensions, pathnames, dummy URLs, user input, and Twitter handles. Here is an example: "Double-click the `ideaIC.dmg` or `ideaIU.dmg` file you have downloaded to mount the macOS disk image."

A block of code is set as follows:

```
repositories {
    maven {
        url 'https://repo.spring.io/libs-milestone'
    }
}
dependencies {
    compile 'org.springframework:spring-context:5.0.0.RC4'

}
```

When we wish to draw your attention to a particular part of a code block, the relevant lines or items are set in bold:

```
repositories {
    maven {
        url 'https://repo.spring.io/libs-milestone'
    }
}
dependencies {
    compile 'org.springframework:spring-context:5.0.0.RC4'
}
```

Any command-line input or output is written as follows:

```
$ git config --global user.name "Your Name"
$ git config --global user.email "you@example.com"
```

Bold: Indicates a new term, an important word, or words that you see onscreen. For example, words in menus or dialog boxes appear in the text like this. Here is an example: "You can choose between the default theme and the **Darcula** theme."

 Warnings or important notes appear like this.

 Tips and tricks appear like this.

Get in touch

Feedback from our readers is always welcome.

General feedback: Email feedback@packtpub.com and mention the book title in the subject of your message. If you have questions about any aspect of this book, please email us at questions@packtpub.com.

Errata: Although we have taken every care to ensure the accuracy of our content, mistakes do happen. If you have found a mistake in this book, we would be grateful if you would report this to us. Please visit www.packtpub.com/submit-errata, selecting your book, clicking on the Errata Submission Form link, and entering the details.

Piracy: If you come across any illegal copies of our works in any form on the Internet, we would be grateful if you would provide us with the location address or website name. Please contact us at `copyright@packtpub.com` with a link to the material.

If you are interested in becoming an author: If there is a topic that you have expertise in and you are interested in either writing or contributing to a book, please visit `authors.packtpub.com`.

Reviews

Please leave a review. Once you have read and used this book, why not leave a review on the site that you purchased it from? Potential readers can then see and use your unbiased opinion to make purchase decisions, we at Packt can understand what you think about our products, and our authors can see your feedback on their book. Thank you!

For more information about Packt, please visit `packtpub.com`.

Starting Up 1

Welcome! You are starting a long trip into the unknown: the unknown kingdom of Spring Framework. Luckily, you have the right guide and great companions! You have us! In this book, you will discover what Spring Framework is and how powerful it can be in modern web application development. We will teach you all about workflow with the framework and guide you through a real-world application example. Get ready to learn!

This chapter will cover the following points:

- Defining your mission
- Separating code into independent entities
- Planning your environment
- Preparing the working environment
- Setting up a Git repository

What is your mission?

Your mission, as we mentioned, will be making a real-world application. What can be a better learning path than building real things from scratch through to production deployment? Our real-world application example will have a real theme!

We will create a REST application that will represent the **application programming interface (API)** for other applications. The theme for our application will be simple: management for user Notes and TODOs.

Imagine that there is a real-world mobile application that manages all these Notes and TODOs. That application will need a REST API so that all the data is synchronized to the backend. The story is simple. The user creates a Note or TODO. The user's mobile application then, at some point, does the synchronization. After some time, the user updates the content in it. Again, data is synchronized with the remote backend instance. Then, after a year, the user buys a new device that has a plain mobile application running. Luckily, the mobile application will synchronize with the remote backend instance again and get all the Notes and TODOs the user created.

So, what will this REST API do?

It will expose to the end user API calls for all **Create, Read, Update, and Delete** (**CRUD**) operations. The data we create or modify will be stored in the persistence layer. In our case, that will be MySQL database. Using Spring Security, we will create user roles so certain user profiles can do various things, such as creating the other users or modifying the main application content. To make things more interesting, we will create microservices responsible for various tasks.

Before we deploy, we will first test our code with the proper tests. We will also write unit tests. All tests will cover some of the core functionality so that our application is sufficiently stable to be deployed. We will deploy to Apache Tomcat and to Amazon AWS Elastic Beanstalk.

Separating code into independent entities

Before we start with the implementation, we will separate our code into independent entities. Each entity will cover a single responsibility and therefore will be implemented when we cover a certain Spring functionality.

We will start with the main classes that will represent the data we will actually handle: Notes and TODOs. Then we will describe user-related stuff: the users themselves and the roles we plan to assign to them. Later, when we actually implement most of them, we will introduce some new entities to cover additional responsibilities. This will be explained in Chapter 3, *Building Your First Spring RESTful Service with Kotlin*.

Describing entities

The main entities that we will use and that will hold the data are Notes and TODOs. We can consider each of them as an entry that will be stored and that has common attributes:

- `ID`: **Universally Unique IDentifier (UUID)** String
- `Title`: String
- `Message`: String
- `Location`: String value that represents serialized Location class into JSON.

Here are all the entities that we use:

- `Note`: The `Note` entity will represent Notes in the system with all common attributes.
- `TODO`: The `TODO` entity will represent TODOs in the system with all common attributes and timestamps for a scheduled time.
- `User`: The `User` entity will be completely independent of the main data entities. The user will represent the user and all the attributes that the user of the system can have, including assigned roles. The user will have the following attributes:
    - `ID`: UUID String
    - `Email`: String
    - `Password`: String
    - `First name`: String
    - `Last name`: String
    - `Roles`: String
- `Enabled`: Boolean representing whether the user has activated the account or whether it has been activated by the user from a higher user hierarchy
- `Created on`: Long representing UTC timestamp when the user was created
- `Updated on`: Long representing UTC timestamp when the user was updated

In later stages, we can introduce additional attributes if there is a need. For now, we will stick to the most important ones we just described.

Planning your development

For every project you do, for big and complex projects, and for small ones too, planning is crucial! We will plan our development according to the chapter structure of this book. So, some stuff will be done first and some later. As you have probably realized, user-related functionalities will be provided when we touch on Spring Security. Until then, we will be focused on the main data entities and their relationship with Spring Framework and API clients as well.

Before you get into the deep implementation, it would be wise to plan your work first. As we already did, you should identify all your entities and the relations between them. You must be aware of potential hard connections between them. The best scenario is that each entity is completely independent and not aware of others. In our case, the user entity does not have any awareness of our main data entities, Notes, and TODOs, and vice versa.

Then, if we put all this on paper, we can consider what environments we will have. A common practice is that we have development, staging, and production environments. For bigger projects, sometimes a preproduction environment is also used. In our case, we will have a local development environment, too. The local development environment will be the one we will use for all these exercises. We will use our local working machines running an instance of MySQL and our Spring Framework application.

You must plan how will you deploy the application. For example, an application can run on Apache Tomcat or Amazon AWS. These are not the only options available. Depending on your needs, you will choose a proper deployment platform and deployment scenario. We will discuss this in more detail in `Chapter 10`, *Project Deployment*.

Preparing the working environment

Finally, it's time to prepare our working environment. We will prepare all the software needed to develop and run our application. For this process, we will need the following:

- Git
- JDK
- IDE
- Spring 5
- Postman

For a proper development machine, you can use any computer having, for example, an i5 processor (or more powerful) with at least 8 GB of RAM. These are the main characteristics. You can do your development on Microsoft Windows, Linux, or macOS. All the development mentioned in this book was done on macOS Sierra (version 10.12.6).

Installing Git

We will use Git as our version control system. To install it, follow the procedure for your OS. We will provide guidance for the following:

- Microsoft Windows
- Linux (Debian, Ubuntu, Fedora, and raw source code)
- macOS

Microsoft Windows

Here are the steps for installing Git on Microsoft Windows:

1. Download Git for Microsoft Windows from the following location: https://git-for-windows.github.io/.
2. Start the installer and follow the instructions.
3. Open the Command Prompt.
4. Configure Git with the following commands:

```
$ git config --global user.name "Your Name"
$ git config --global user.email "you@example.com"
```

macOS

To install Git on macOS, we recommend that you install Xcode with command-line tools from the App Store. Then, open Terminal and verify the Git version:

```
$ git -version
git version 2.7.0 (Apple Git-66)
```

Linux

Follow the installation steps for your distribution.

Debian and Ubuntu

The following are the steps to install Git on Debian and Ubuntu:

1. Open Terminal.
2. Use the following commands to start the installation:

    ```
    $ sudo apt-get update
    $ sudo apt-get install git
    ```

3. Verify the installation:

    ```
    $ git -version
    ```

    The output should be something like the following:

    ```
    git version 2.9.2
    ```

4. Configure Git with the following commands:

    ```
    $ git config --global user.name "Your Name"
    $ git config --global user.email "you@example.com"
    ```

Fedora

The following are the steps to install Git on Fedora:

1. Open Terminal.
2. Depending on your Fedora version, use YUM or DNF to install Git as follows:

    ```
    $ sudo dnf install git
    //or
    $ sudo yum install git
    ```

3. Verify the installation:

    ```
    $ git -version
    ```

The output should be something like the following:

```
git version 2.9.2
```

4. Configure Git with the following commands:

```
$ git config --global user.name "Your Name"
$ git config --global user.email "you@example.com"
```

Building Git from the source code

If you prefer to build your stuff from source code, you can do the same with Git.

Debian and Ubuntu

To build from source, you need some dependencies installed:

1. Open Terminal and install the following dependencies:

```
$ sudo apt-get update
$ sudo apt-get install libcurl4-gnutls-dev libexpat1-dev gettext
libz-dev libssl-dev asciidoc xmlto docbook2x
```

2. Navigate to your preferred directory.
3. Clone the Git source code as follows:

```
$ git clone https://git.kernel.org/pub/scm/git/git.git
```

4. Build Git as follows:

```
$ make all doc info prefix=/usr
$ sudo make install install-doc install-html install-info install-
man prefix=/usr
```

We installed Git in the /usr directory. Use a different filesystem location if you prefer.

Fedora

The following are the steps to build from the source code:

1. As was the case with Debian and Ubuntu, install the dependencies needed to build Git as follows:

```
$ sudo dnf install curl-devel expat-devel gettext-devel openssl-
devel perl-devel zlib-devel asciidoc xmlto docbook2X
```

   If you have an older version of Fedora, run the following commands:

```
$ sudo yum install epel-release
$ sudo yum install curl-devel expat-devel gettext-devel openssl-
devel perl-devel zlib-devel asciidoc xmlto docbook2X
```

2. Symlink `docbook2X` to the filename that the Git build expects:

```
$ sudo ln -s /usr/bin/db2x_docbook2texi /usr/bin/docbook2x-texi
```

3. Navigate to your preferred directory.
4. Clone the Git source code as follows:

```
$git clone https://git.kernel.org/pub/scm/git/git.git
```

5. Finally, build Git:

```
$ make all doc prefix=/usr
$ sudo make install install-doc install-html install-man
prefix=/usr
```

We installed Git in the /usr directory. Use a different filesystem location if you prefer.

Congratulations! You have installed the Git version control system on your machine! You are ready to create repositories that will keep your code. We will do this in *Setting up a Git repository* section.

Installing JDK

As you already know, we will use Kotlin as our primary development language. However, we need Java installed on our system since Kotlin is executed on JVM. Open the Java JDK home page and chose the proper installation depending on the version of your OS: `http://www.oracle.com/technetwork/java/javase/downloads/jdk8-downloads-2133151.html`.

The following platforms are supported:

- Linux ARM 32 Hard Float ABI
- Linux ARM 64 Hard Float ABI
- Linux x86
- Linux x86
- Linux x64
- Linux x64
- macOS X
- Solaris SPARC 64-bit
- Solaris SPARC 64-bit
- Solaris x64
- Solaris x64
- Windows x86
- Windows x64

Follow the instructions depending on your OS version.

Microsoft Windows

The following are the steps to install JDK in Microsoft Windows:

1. Download the proper executable for your version of Microsoft Windows
2. Execute the downloaded file
3. Follow the instructions

Linux

Here are the steps to install JDK in Linux:

1. Download the proper **RPM Package Manager** (**RPM**) installation package for your platform.
2. Open Terminal and install the package:

   ```
   $ rpm -ihv package_you_downloaded.rpm
   ```

3. Verify you have installed the Java version:

   ```
   $ java -version
   ```

macOS

The following are the steps to install JDK in macOS:

1. Download the dmg file for your macOS.
2. Double-click on the dmg file to run it.
3. Double-click on the PKG icon to launch the installation.
4. Follow the installation instructions. Enter your system credentials if asked.
5. Verify that the Java version from Terminal:

   ```
   $ java -version
   java version "1.8.0_144"
   Java(TM) SE Runtime Environment (build 1.8.0_144-b01)
   Java HotSpot(TM) 64-Bit Server VM (build 25.144-b01, mixed mode)
   ```

Congratulations! Java is up and running! The next thing we are going to do is set up our IDE.

Installing the IDE

We chose IntelliJ IDEA as our IDE. Unfortunately, IDEA is not free. It is commercial software. You can buy a license or use IntelliJ IDEA Community Edition, Eclipse, or NetBeans to get it running. Follow the installation instructions for your specific OS.

Microsoft Windows

The following are the steps to install IDEA in Microsoft Windows:

1. Download IntelliJ IDEA from the JetBrains website: `https://www.jetbrains.com/idea/download/#section=windows`.
2. Launch setup by executing the file you downloaded.
3. Follow the installation instructions.

Linux

The following are the steps to install IDEA in Linux:

1. Download IntelliJ IDEA from the JetBrains website: `https://www.jetbrains.com/idea/download/#section=linux`.
2. Unpack the `ideaIC.gz` or `ideaIU.gz` file you have downloaded.
3. Switch to the directory where you extracted IntelliJ IDEA.
4. Execute the `idea.sh` script.

macOS

The following are the steps to install IDEA in macOS:

1. Download IntelliJ IDEA from the JetBrains website: `https://www.jetbrains.com/idea/download/#section=macos`.
2. Double-click the `ideaIC.dmg` or `ideaIU.dmg` file you have downloaded to mount the macOS disk image.
3. Copy IntelliJ IDEA to the `Applications` folder.

Starting IntelliJ for the first time

You have installed IntelliJ; now it is time for the first run. You will be asked to do some configuring. Don't worry, everything is simple and easy. Just follow the instructions:

1. Launch IntelliJ and wait until the **Complete Installation** dialog appears. Choose **Don't import settings** and continue by clicking on **OK**.

2. Next, you will be prompted to select the UI theme. You can choose between the default theme and the **Darcula** theme. We recommend that you use the **Darcula** theme:

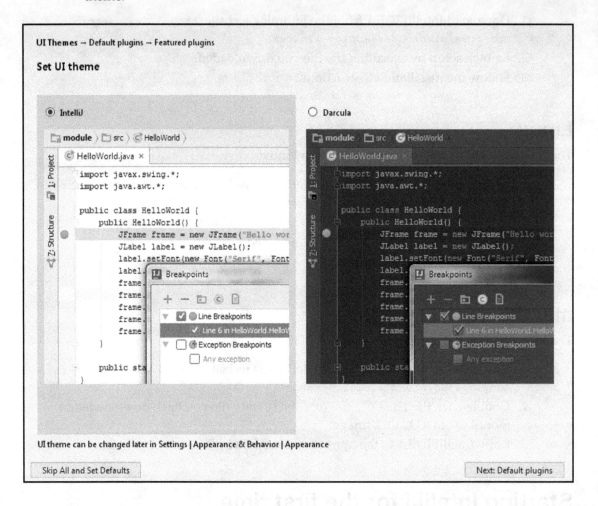

3. In the next section, disable any plugins that are not required:

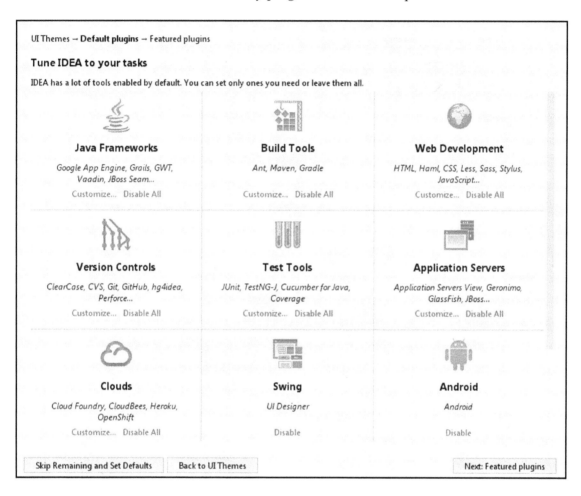

4. In the next step, you are prompted to download additional plugins:

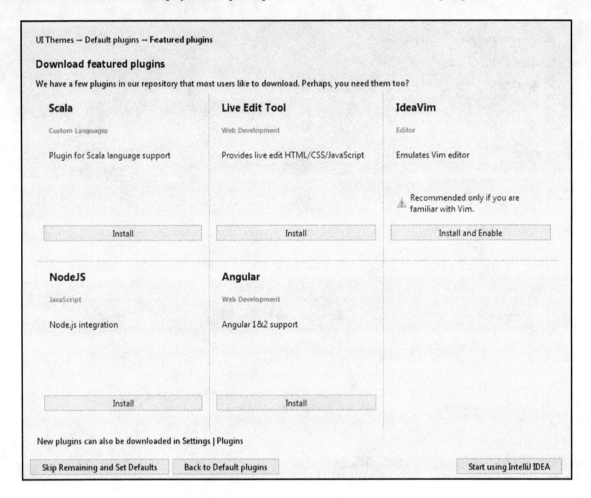

5. Finally, you can start the project! The setup is complete, as shown in the following screenshot:

Installing Spring 5

Before installing or running Spring 5, we need to install Kotlin, since this is our primary programming language for the project:

1. Open IntelliJ IDEA and choose **Configure** | **Plugins**, as shown in the following screenshot:

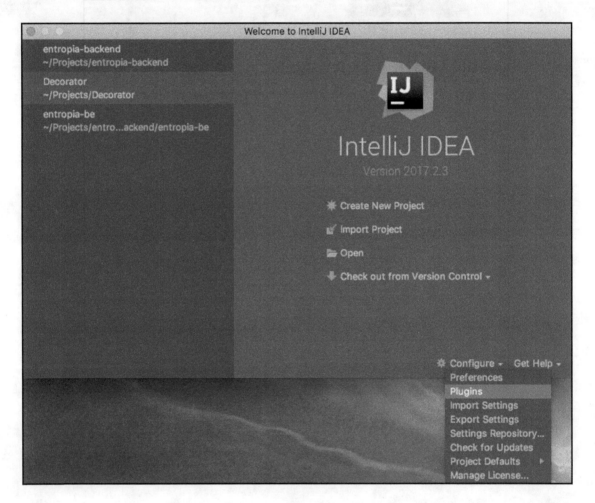

2. In the search field, type `Kotlin`:

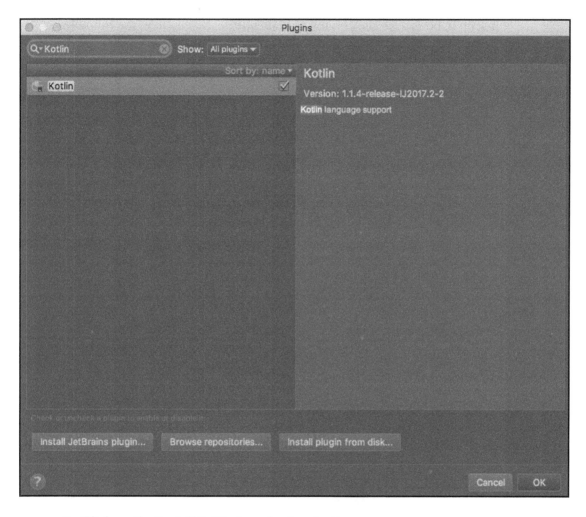

3. Click on the **Install JetBrains plugin...** button.

4. From the list that appears, choose **Kotlin**.

If you do not already have Kotlin installed, you will see a green **Install** button. Click on it, otherwise click on the **Update** button, as shown in the following screenshot:

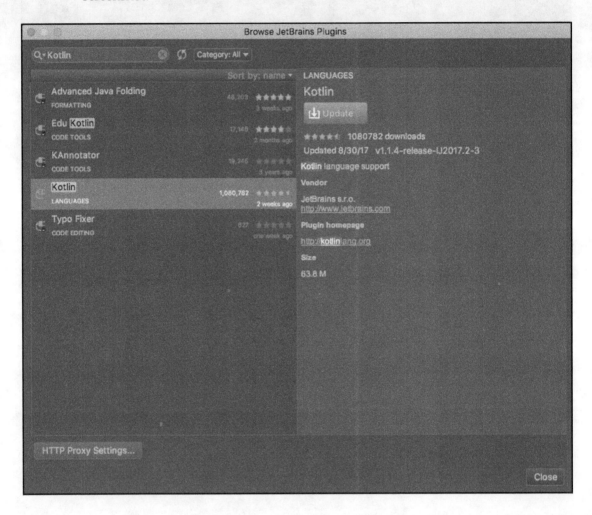

5. Wait until the installation or update process completes:

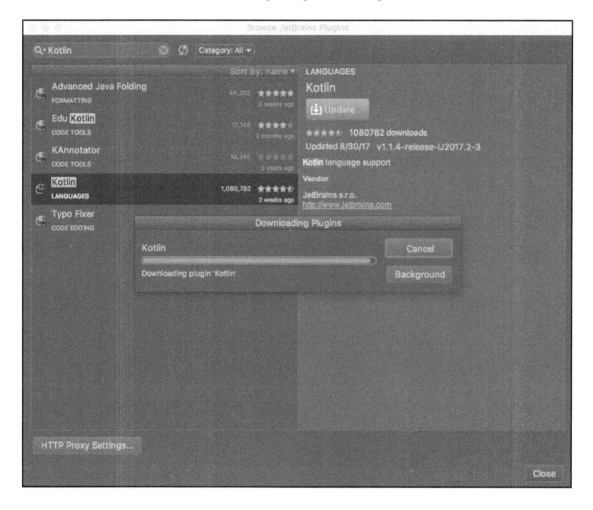

6. When the installation is finished, click on the **Restart IntelliJ IDEA** button:

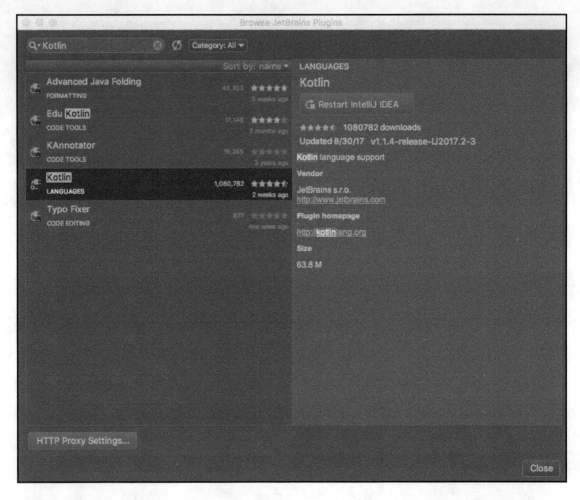

If the **Restart IntelliJ IDEA** button does not restart your IDE, do it yourself manually.

Your IDE is ready for development. It is time to finally set up Spring 5! You can use Spring in the same way as any standard Java library. Simply include the appropriate Spring library files in your classpath. Spring does not require any special tool integration, so you can use any IDE or text editor! As you already know, we will stick to IntelliJ IDEA. You can run and debug Spring applications as you would any other Java application.

Spring can be used through Maven or Gradle. It is up to you to choose which suits you better. We will use Gradle in our development but we will give examples of Maven too.

Maven installation

The recommended way to get started using Spring Framework in your project is with a dependency management system. Take a look at the following Maven example:

```
<dependencies>
    <dependency>
        <groupId>org.springframework</groupId>
        <artifactId>spring-context</artifactId>
        <version>5.0.0.RC4</version>
    </dependency>
</dependencies><repositories>
    <repository>
        <id>spring-milestones</id>
        <name>Spring Milestones</name>
        <url>https://repo.spring.io/libs-milestone</url>
        <snapshots>
            <enabled>false</enabled>
        </snapshots>
    </repository>
</repositories>
```

Gradle installation

Gradle installation requires less code, as the following snippet shows:

```
repositories {
    maven {
        url 'https://repo.spring.io/libs-milestone'
    }
}
dependencies {
    compile 'org.springframework:spring-context:5.0.0.RC4'

}
```

Installing Postman

To try out our API calls, we will need Postman. Postman is a complete toolchain for API development. Postman is designed from the ground up to support the API developer. It offers us an intuitive user interface to send requests, save responses, add tests, and create workflows.

To get Postman, open `https://www.getpostman.com/postman` and choose your OS.

Microsoft Windows installation

The following are the steps to install Postman in Microsoft Windows:

1. Download the setup file
2. Run the installer
3. Follow the setup instructions

Linux installation

To simplify the installation process, we recommend that you install it through the Google Chrome store. Search for Postman and install it:

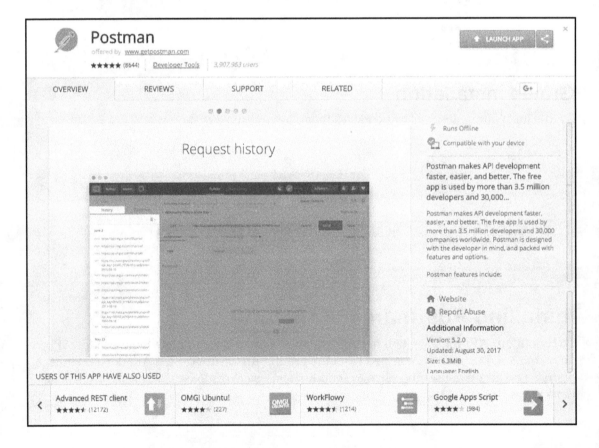

macOS installation

Once you have downloaded the Postman-archived application, extract it, then drag the file to the `Applications` folder. Double-click on **Postman** to open the application.

Postman is installed. Run it and take a look at its UI. We will not go into details on how to use it. It is enough to play a bit. Most of the options are self-explanatory. Enjoy!

The following screenshot shows the Postman application running on macOS:

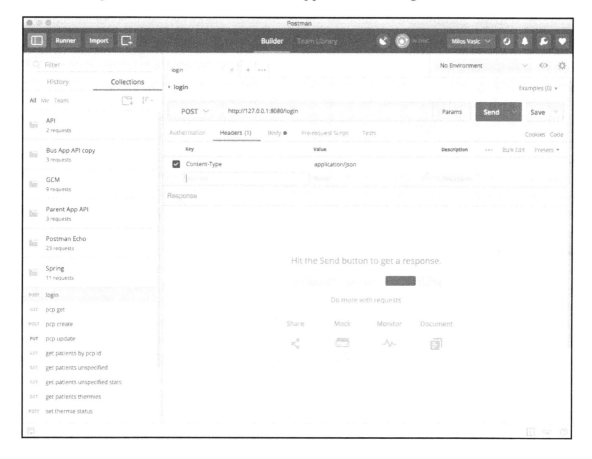

Setting up a Git repository

We have installed the IDE and Spring Framework. It is time to start working on our project. We will develop a REST application API for Notes and TODOs. This is a tool that everybody needs. We will give it a name: Journaler API. Journaler API will be a REST application capable of creating Notes and TODOs with reminders. Many different applications, such as mobile ones, will be synced to our backend instance running this REST application.

The first step in development is initializing a Git repository. Git will be our code versioning system. It is up to you to decide whether you will use GitHub, BitBucket, or something else for your remote Git instance. Create your remote repository and keep its URL ready along with your credentials. So, let's start!

The following are the steps to set up Git:

1. Go into the directory containing the project.
2. Execute the following command:

   ```
   $ git init .
   ```

   The console output will be something like the following:

   ```
   Initialized empty Git repository in <directory_you_choose/.git>
   ```

3. We have initialized the repository. Now let's add the first file by executing the following command:

   ```
   $ vi notes.txt
   ```

    Here we are using vi editor to edit notes.txt. If you are familiar with some other editor, use that.

4. Populate notes.txt with some content and save it.
5. To add all of the relevant files, execute the following commands:

   ```
   $ git add .
   $ git commit -m "Journaler API: First commit"
   ```

The console output will be something like the following:

```
[master (root-commit) 5e98ea4] Journaler API: First commit

1 file changed, 1 insertion(+)

create mode 100644 notes.txt
```

6. Use the remote Git repository URL that you have prepared previously with credentials, and execute the following command:

```
$ git remote add origin <repository_url>
```

This sets the new remote.

7. Execute the following command to verify the new remote URL:

```
$ git remote -v
```

8. Finally, push everything we have to remote, by executing the following command:

```
$ git push -u origin master
```

If you are asked for credentials, enter them and confirm by pressing *Enter*.

Summary

These are exciting times! We are preparing to dive deep into the depths of Spring Framework. We are practically ready! We have set our environment up! We have installed Git, Java JDK, and IDE, shown you how Spring Framework is installed, and finally installed Postman. We skipped the MySQL installation for now but we will get back to it once we introduce you to Spring data.

Dear reader, we have come to the end of the first chapter. We have learned how to set up and configure the environment for development. In the next chapter, we will make our first real steps into Spring Framework. We will explain what Spring is and why you need it! We will write some code, run it, and trigger our first API call. So, get ready!

Starting with Spring

2

In the previous chapter, we set up our development environment. We are now ready to create our first Spring code written in Kotlin. To do that, we will get familiar with Spring background and explain what exactly Spring can do. When we introduce you to Spring background, we will kick off the project! Get ready!

In this chapter, we will learn the following:

- What is Spring?
- Spring's most important features
- Kotlin support for Spring
- Generating projects
- Creating Spring project in IntelliJ

What is Spring?

The Spring Framework is a framework developed by the Pivotal company. The framework offers to end the user's programming and configuration model for modern enterprise applications. Spring Framework is made for developers to be able to focus on application-level business logic. Today almost all modern enterprise applications are developed by using Spring Framework. That makes it one of the most widely used and popular development frameworks available.

What features does it offer?

Spring Framework comes with plenty of modern features every developer needs. Here, we will highlight the most important ones and say a few words about them.

Dependency injection

When we talk about the Spring Framework here, the first thing we need to mention is dependency injection. This is a useful feature that is required in everyday development. Every developer tries to create classes that are as independent as possible. Developers try to create a system where classes are not aware of each other, that is—they are loosely coupled. Dependency injection helps developers in wiring those classes together and, at the same time, keeping them independent.

How do we achieve this?

In modern software development, dependency injection is a technique where object A provides the dependencies for another object, object B. So, the dependency is this provided object. Injection represents a dependency providing a mechanism to a dependent object that would use it. A good use case example could be providing dependencies for unit testing.

A common way of providing decencies is by creating a `dependency` instance or by using a `factory` object to make one instance for them. By using dependency injection, an instance is passed to the *client* externally. Passing that is somebody else's problem, not yours! So, who is this *somebody else*? This *somebody* is one of the following:

- An object higher in the dependency graph
- A dependency injector (framework) that creates our dependency graph

We will now show you some examples of dependency injection. We will show you examples of injection through the constructor and through the use of a factory. In both cases, things can become complicated if we plan to do some serious testing. Spring Framework makes it easy for us! We will show you how in the next chapters of the book.

Injection through the constructor should look like this:

```
class MyExampleClass(val parameter: Any){
    private val dependency: Any
    init {
        dependency = parameter
        // Do some work dependency related
    }
}

Injection using the factory would look like this:
class MyExampleClass2 {
    private val dependency = Factory().create()
}

class Factory {
```

```
    fun create(): Any {
        // To some instantiation work
        return Any()
    }
}
```

As we mentioned, a good example of using dependency injection is when we plan to do testing. Dependency injection will make testing much simpler and easier! So, what problems can arise from these two examples? Let's say you attempt to do the testing for `MyExampleClass2`. We need a mock (or stub) class version. A bigger complication is when we can't easily influence the `Factory` class! An easier approach would be to use constructor injection. But, that does not solve the problem. Why? Circular dependency between two objects constructed like this is not an option anymore. This is not the case with dependency injection through setters. Soon, you will notice that the cons associated with this design approach will outweigh the pros!

Inversion of Control (IoC)

The most important mechanism responsible for achieving loose coupling is the IoC. What does this mean? Dependent objects give their own dependencies instead of creating or looking for dependent objects. IoC is a technique in which object coupling is bound at runtime by assembler that performs object coupling. Both IoC and dependency injection patterns are mechanisms responsible for removing dependencies from your code base.

Let's provide some examples to illustrate this. Imagine an application that has a music player and you need to provide it with a volume control mechanism. We will start with this:

```
class VolumeControl
class MusicPlayer {
    val volumeControl = VolumeControl()
}
```

Now, let's do the IoC on it:

```
abstract class VolumeControlAbstract
class MusicPlayerIOC(
        private val volumeControl: VolumeControlAbstract
)
```

In the first code example, we are instantiating class:

```
val volumeControl = VolumeControl()
```

Which means the `MusicPlayer` class depends directly on the `VolumeControl` class!

What about the second example? In the second example, we are creating an abstraction. We defined the `VolumeControl` dependency class in the `MusicPlayer` constructor signature. In this example, we do not initialize dependency in the class itself. We call the dependency and pass it to the `MusicPlayer` class as follows:

```
// Init. dependency.
val vc = VolumeControlImpl()

// Pass dependency.
val player = MusicPlayerIOC(vc)
```

In this example, the client creating the `MusicPlayer` class instance has control over the `VolumeControl` implementation you will use. As you can see, we are injecting the dependency to the `MusicPlayer` class signature!

Aspect Oriented Programming (AOP)

Spring has one more important key component: the AOP Framework. AOP provides object-oriented programming API. AOP provides another way of thinking about program structure. What does it mean? The key unit of modularity in object-oriented programming is the class. Aspect represents the unit of modularity in AOP. Dependency injection is used to decouple application objects from each other. On the other hand, AOP helps you to decouple cross-cutting concerns from the objects that they affect. A cross-cutting concern can be described as any functionality that affects multiple points of an application. A good example of this can be *security*. Why? Because many methods in an application can have security rules applied to them.

Thanks to AOP, each module provides an AOP implementation. In the chapters that follow, we will use AOP in real code examples.

Container

A good thing about the Spring Framework is that it creates and manages the life cycle and the configuration of application objects. For that purpose, we have the `org.springframework.context.ApplicationContext` interface available. This interface is responsible for instantiating, configuring, and assembling beans. With Spring Framework, we have a couple of implementations of `ApplicationContext` available out of the box.

MVC framework

Spring Framework provides an MVC web application framework. What does this mean? MVC can be configured through interfaces also, and it accommodates multiple view technologies. **Model-View-Controller** (**MVC**) makes development easy and clean. MVC is a software architectural pattern for implementing user interfaces on computers. The pattern divides our application into three parts, as its name says: model, view, and the controller.

Model

This is the central component of the pattern. Model expresses an application's behavior in terms of the problem domain that is independent of the user interface. Model directly affects the data, application logic, and their rules.

View

This is the output representation of the information our application is handling. A good example can be an HTML page as a final result of our API call. Here, we are not limited to a single view! With MVC, multiple views of the same information are possible.

Controller

This accepts the input data and converts it to commands for the model or the view. As you can see, this is one more example of decoupling in the Spring Framework!

Transaction management

For transaction management, Spring Framework provides a generic abstraction layer. Transaction management is not tied to J2EE environments. Unlike EJB CMT, which is tied to JTA, the Spring Framework's declarative transaction management works in any environment. Spring Transaction Management can work with JTA transactions or, if needed, with local transactions, using:

- JDBC
- JPA
- Hibernate
- JDO

All this simply by adjusting the configuration files!

Misc

In Spring Framework, the JDBC abstraction layer offers an exception hierarchy. This simplifies the error handling strategy.

Spring Framework gives you the ability to develop enterprise-class applications using POJOs. What is the benefit? The benefit of using POJOs is that you do not need an EJB container product such as an application server. A developer has the option of using only a robust servlet container, such as Tomcat or some other commercial product. AWS can be one of the possible solutions.

It's important to note that Spring Framework is organized in a modular way which means that you have to think only about the packages you need and ignore the others.

With Spring Framework, you can use some of the most popular technologies such as misc ORM Frameworks, logging frameworks, JEE, Quartz, and JDK timers, as well as many other view technologies.

What about the testing? Testing applications in Spring Framework is simple and easy. Environment-dependent code is moved into this framework. By using Java bean-style POJOs, it is easy to use dependency injection for injecting test data.

Spring Framework provides a great API to translate technology-specific exceptions into consistent, unchecked exceptions for end users.

Spring's IoC containers are lightweight. If we compare it to EJB containers, the difference is significant. Thanks to this, we will spend less memory and CPU power.

These are some of the most frequently highlighted features of Spring. You will encounter each during a journey of this book. Also, you will spot some others that we did not mention, but in general, once you dive into Spring, you will not want to try any other framework for a very, very long time! Probably never!

How well is Kotlin supported?

Starting from version 5, Spring Framework officially supports Kotlin. This is great news! One of the key strengths of Kotlin is that it provides very good interoperability with libraries written in Java. And that is not all! Now we can write fully idiomatic Kotlin code when developing Spring applications. With Kotlin and Spring 5, we are attaining a completely new level of productivity and flexibility! Because of this, support for Kotlin has finally been introduced in Spring Framework 5.

Key features that allow Kotlin and Spring to work together are Kotlin extensions. Using Kotlin extensions, it's possible to extend existing APIs. With the latest version of Spring Framework, everything reaches a new dimension!

It's important to note that Kotlin extensions are statically resolved. You must import them.

Let's highlight some of the benefits that Kotlin is bringing to Spring development:

- Spring now takes advantage of Kotlin null-safety support.
- Spring Framework 5 comes with a Kotlin-routing DSL.
- Kotlin reified type parameters provide a workaround for JVM generics type erasure.
- Kotlin-based Gradle build configuration.
- Kotlin Script-based templates.
- Combining Spring Framework with Kotlin allows us to write applications more efficiently, and more simply with expressive, short and readable code. Spring support for Kotlin is an important step in future development for all developers who use Spring!

Creating Spring project

The time has come to create our first Spring code and run it. We will, of course, use Kotlin as our primary development language. For project initialization, we will use Spring Initializr.

What is Spring Initializr?

In one sentence, Spring Initializr is a web-based quick start generator for Spring Framework projects. You can access it online at the following URL:

```
https://start.spring.io/
```

And from it's GitHub repository, `https://github.com/spring-io/initializr`, since it's open an source project.

Spring Initializr provides API to generate quick start Spring Framework projects. You can use the default instance hosted on the `spring.io` domain or clone the GitHub repository and host your own instance.

Initializr offers a configuration structure. With a configuration structure, you can define all aspects of the project that you plan to generate. For example:

- A list of dependencies
- A supported Java version
- A supported Kotlin version
- A boot version, and so on

Generating the project

Open your browser on the Initializr landing page:

```
https://start.spring.io/
```

As you can see, the configuration wizard appears as shown in the following screenshot:

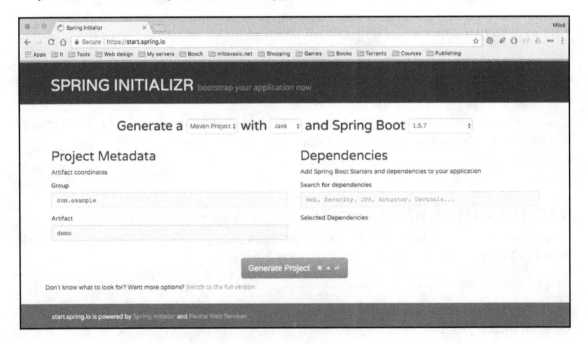

We will configure our project like this:

- Generate a **Gradle Project** with **Kotlin** and Spring Boot **2.0.0 M4**
- Set the **Group** project to com.journaler
- Set the **Artifact** project to api

The following screenshot shows the project configuration:

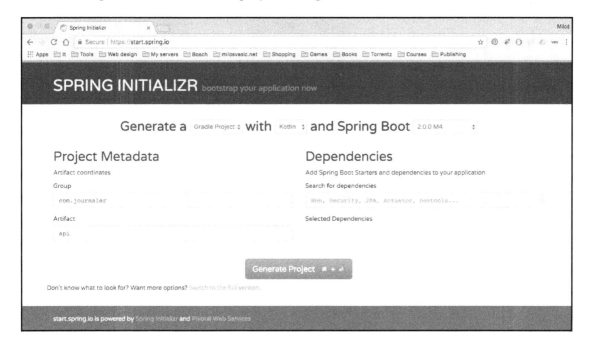

We will keep our first configuration simple and extend it later as we progress and need more dependencies. Press the **Generate Project** button. You will be asked to save the archive as shown in the following screenshot:

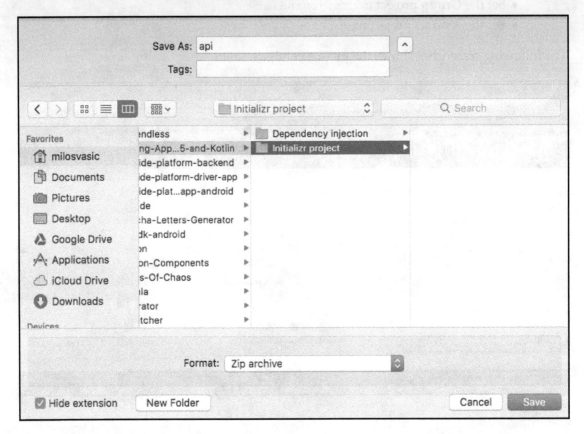

Save `api.zip` to your preferred directory. Open the directory and expand it. Let's have a look at its content in the following screenshot:

This is obviously a standard Gradle Kotlin project and a standard application. We will take a detailed look at the most important files the project contains. Open your `build.gradle` configuration. It should have content very similar to this:

```
buildscript {
    ext {
        kotlinVersion = '1.1.4-3'
        springBootVersion = '2.0.0.M4'
    }
    repositories {
        mavenCentral()
        maven { url "https://repo.spring.io/snapshot" }
        maven { url "https://repo.spring.io/milestone" }
    }
    dependencies {
        classpath("org.springframework.boot:spring-boot-gradle-
        plugin:${springBootVersion}")
        classpath("org.jetbrains.kotlin:kotlin-gradle-
plugin:${kotlinVersion}")
        classpath("org.jetbrains.kotlin:kotlin-allopen:${kotlinVersion}")
    }
}
```

```
apply plugin: 'kotlin'
apply plugin: 'kotlin-spring'
apply plugin: 'eclipse'
apply plugin: 'org.springframework.boot'
apply plugin: 'io.spring.dependency-management'

group = 'com.journaler'
version = '0.0.1-SNAPSHOT'
ssourceCompatibility = 1.8
compileKotlin {
    kotlinOptions.jvmTarget = "1.8"
}
compileTestKotlin {
    kotlinOptions.jvmTarget = "1.8"
}

repositories {
    mavenCentral()
    maven { url "https://repo.spring.io/snapshot" }
    maven { url "https://repo.spring.io/milestone" }
}

dependencies {
    compile('org.springframework.boot:spring-boot-starter')
    compile("org.jetbrains.kotlin:kotlin-stdlib-jre8:${kotlinVersion}")
    compile("org.jetbrains.kotlin:kotlin-reflect:${kotlinVersion}")
    testCompile('org.springframework.boot:spring-boot-starter-test')
}
```

Going from top to bottom, the script does the following for our project:

- It defines Kotlin and Spring Boot versions
- It defines build script repositories and classpaths
- It applies Gradle plugins needed for the application to build and run
- It defines project group as `com.journaler`
- It defines version as 1.0 snapshot
- It set Kotlin's JVM compatibility to 1.8
- It defines project dependency repositories
- It defines Kotlin and Spring dependencies

The next important aspect for us is the Git ignore configuration. Open `.gitignore` and take a look:

```
.gradle
/build/
!gradle/wrapper/gradle-wrapper.jar

### STS ###
.apt_generated
.classpath
.factorypath
.project
.settings
.springBeans

### IntelliJ IDEA ###
.idea
*.iws
*.iml
*.ipr

### NetBeans ###
nbproject/private/
build/
nbbuild/
dist/
nbdist/
.nb-gradle/
```

The `.gitignore` configuration will prevent us to from versioning some unwanted files. Next, open the `application.propeties` file located under the `src/main.resources` directory. The file will be empty. Here, we will define environment-specific parameters for our application.

Finally, let's explore the code! Since this is a Kotlin application, expand the `src/main/kotlin` directory. Continue through the packages structure `com/journaler/api` and open `ApiApplication.kt`:

```
package com.journaler.api

import org.springframework.boot.SpringApplication
import org.springframework.boot.autoconfigure.SpringBootApplication

@SpringBootApplication
class ApiApplication
```

```
fun main(args: Array<String>) {
    SpringApplication.run(ApiApplication::class.java, *args)
}
```

There is not much code in it. The code is simple and easy to understand. We defined the application class called `ApiApplication` and annotation assigned to `SpringBootApplication`. Main application method run Spring application. That's it!

Before we build and run our code, there is one more thing left to check. Expand the directory structure to include the `ApiApplicationTest.kt` test:

```
package com.journaler.api

import org.junit.Test
import org.junit.runner.RunWith
import org.springframework.boot.test.context.SpringBootTest
import org.springframework.test.context.junit4.SpringRunner

@RunWith(SpringRunner::class)
@SpringBootTest
class ApiApplicationTests {
    @Test
    fun contextLoads() {
    }
}
```

In practical terms, this test does not do anything. More information about Spring tests and testing can be found in later chapters of this book. For now, it's enough just to observe the code.

We will build and run our application. Open the Terminal and navigate to the application root directory. Then execute the Gradle clean command:

```
$ ./gradlew clean
```

Gradle starts downloading the required dependencies:

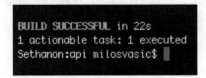

```
BUILD SUCCESSFUL in 22s
1 actionable task: 1 executed
Sethanon:api milosvasic$
```

As you can see, the build completed successfully. To build the application, execute the following command:

```
$ ./gradlew build
```

The code will give the following output:

As you can see, the Gradle task completed successfully. To run the project, navigate to `build/libs` from the Terminal and execute the following command:

```
$ java -jar ./api-0.0.1-SNAPSHOT.jar
```

The code output looks like this:

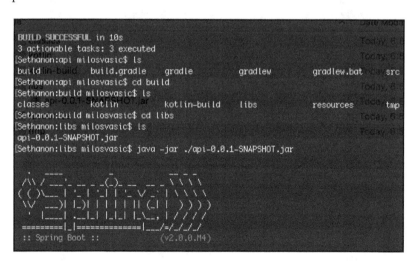

The program will run and show some messages. For now, we will not get into details since we have a long way in front of us before we actually execute the first API call.

For the end of this section, before we create a project from scratch from IntelliJ, we will import this project. Start IntelliJ and choose **Import Project**. Choose the root directory where we extracted the project and confirm by clicking **OK**. The **Import Project** wizard appears. Make sure that the **Create project from existing sources** option is selected. Then, click on **Next**, as shown in the following screenshot:

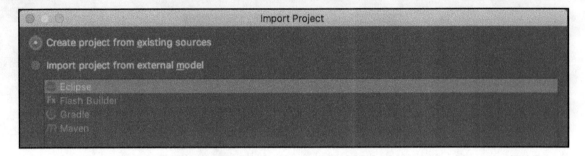

If you are fine with the **Project name** and the path as shown in the following screenshot, click **Next**:

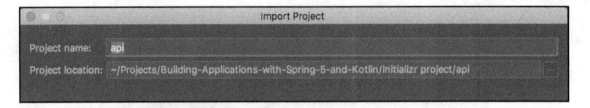

Click **Mark All** and then click **Next**, as shown in the following screenshot:

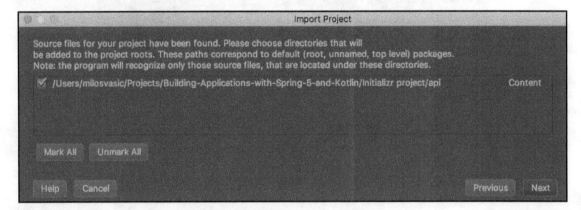

Then click **Finish**, as shown in the following screenshot:

Then, select **Import Gradle project** and add **VCS root** if asked, as shown in the following screenshot:

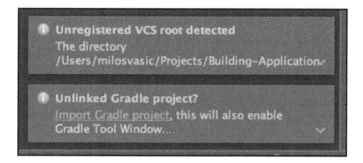

Please use the Gradle wrapper when asked. Confirm the import by clicking on **OK**, as shown in the following screenshot:

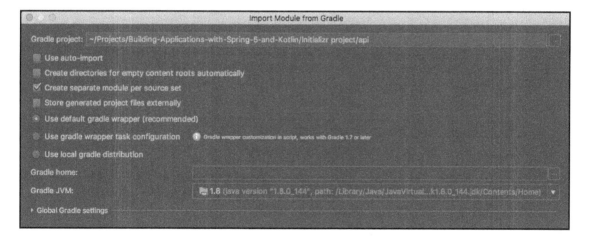

After some time, the project is imported. You will notice that **ApiApplication** is available as the configuration you can run, as shown in the following screenshot:

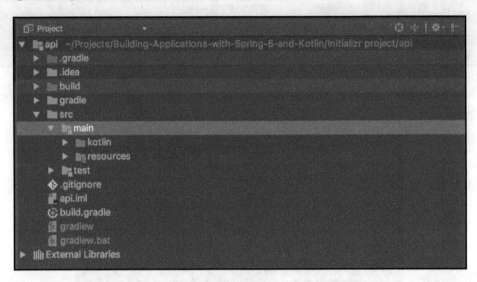

In the event that your IDE does not detect the configuration automatically, run the application by expanding the project and locating `ApiApplication.kt`, then right-click on it and choose Run `ApiApplication.kt`. The output is identical to the last time when we executed JAR.

Add the following lines to your `.gitignore` file so that Gradle wrapper is not versioned. Initializr will not generate those lines:

```
...
gradlew
gradlew.bat
gradle/*
```

Creating Spring project with IntelliJ

To close this chapter, we will demonstrate how to initialize the project from IntelliJ Idea. We will get pretty much the same result as with Initializr. Start IntelliJ and select the **Create new project** option. A **New Project** dialog box appears, as shown in the following screenshot:

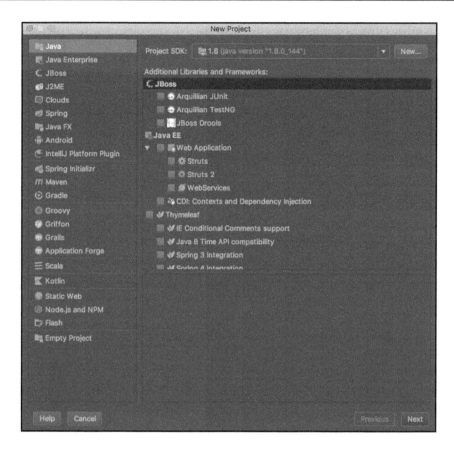

Set your project options, and then select the **Spring** Framework components as shown in the following screenshot:

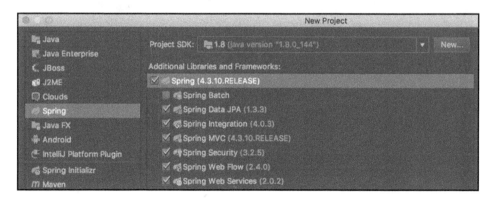

Also, select **Kotlin/JVM** as the language we will use, as shown in the following screenshot:

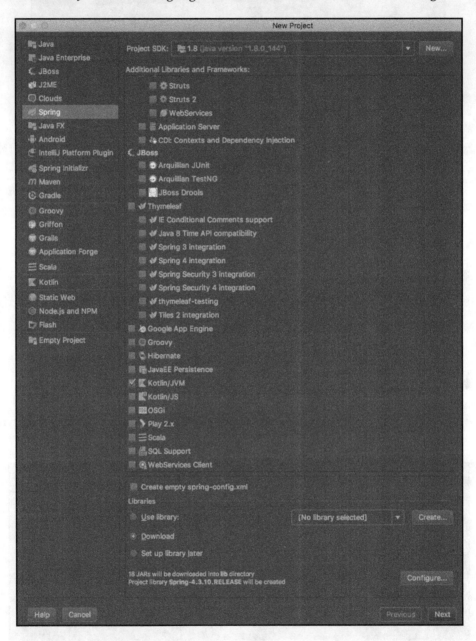

Follow the wizard until the project is ready. You will be asked to enable annotations, as shown in the following screenshot. Please do so!

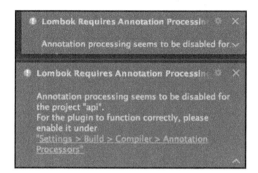

In the following screenshot, you have probably noticed that there is no Spring 5 available as an option, so we will stick to Initializr project initialization since it supports everything we want:

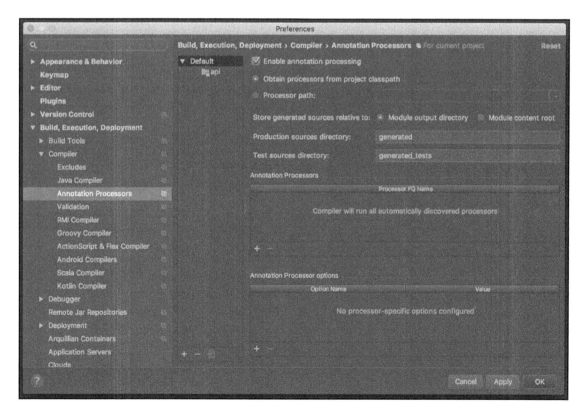

Summary

In this chapter, we introduced you to Spring Framework and its features. We kicked off our first project and successfully performed building and execution. In the next chapter, we will continue our journey and do some more concrete work. We will create our first RESTful service with the controller, data class, and service components.

3
Building Your First Spring RESTful Service with Kotlin

In the previous chapter, we just started our Spring application. As you can see, it runs and it stops. This is because we did not implement anything in our application to work with. You will also have noticed that when you start the application, one of the noticeable logs says `:: Spring Boot ::`. That is because we use Spring Boot to run the application. Spring Boot is a framework that we will use to simplify the bootstrapping and development of an application. It frees developers from the need to define a boilerplate configuration.

As we have already said, when we run our Spring application, Spring Boot starts and terminates since there is nothing to do. In this chapter, we will define some things. We will create our first implementation!

Here, you will learn about the following topics:

- Defining dependencies for our project
- Our first controller
- Adding a data class
- Adding an `@Service` component

Defining dependencies for our project

We need to add several dependencies to our project. The first one that we need is the Spring Context dependency. We also need Spring AOP, Boot Starter Web, Actuator, Spring Web, and Spring Web MVC. The application is virtually naked, so let's extend our dependencies:

```
...
dependencies {
    compile 'org.springframework:spring-context'
```

```
compile 'org.springframework:spring-aop'
compile('org.springframework.boot:spring-boot-starter')
compile('org.springframework.boot:spring-boot-starter-web')
compile 'org.springframework.boot:spring-boot-starter-actuator'
compile 'org.springframework:spring-web'
compile 'org.springframework:spring-webmvc'
compile("org.jetbrains.kotlin:kotlin-stdlib-jre8:${kotlinVersion}")
compile("org.jetbrains.kotlin:kotlin-reflect:${kotlinVersion}")
testCompile('org.springframework.boot:spring-boot-starter-test')
}
...
```

 These dependencies are crucial!

Spring Context will provide our application with the following:

- Core support for dependency injection
- Core support for transaction management
- Core support for web applications
- Core support for data access
- Core support for messaging
- Core support for testing
- Miscellaneous

Spring AOP will provide us with support for aspect-oriented programming.

Spring Actuator is a sub-project of Spring Boot. It adds several important services to your Spring application. When the Actuator is configured in your Spring Boot application, you can perform interaction and monitor your application behavior by executing misc HTTP endpoints exposed by Spring Boot Actuator. Actuator offers the following out-of-the-box endpoints:

- Application health
- Bean details
- Version details
- Configurations
- Logger details, and many more

Spring Web and Web MVC will provide our application with access to Spring MVC, request mapping, and all related features. It's important to note that since we didn't perform a test, it is thanks to the Spring Boot Gradle plugin that we achieved the following benefits:

- Collecting all JARs on the classpath and building a single, runnable JAR
- Searching for the `main()` application method to flag as a runnable class that is an entry point to our application
- Providing a dependency resolver that sets the version number to match Spring Boot dependencies

In addition to this, Spring Boot Starter Web (`spring-boot-starter-web`) adds the dependencies needed for building web applications. This includes RESTful applications using Spring MVC, which is exactly what we need. Tomcat is used as the default embedded container for our application. Without it, we wouldn't be able to run our application.

Our first controller

What is a controller? You remember we said that one of the major Spring Framework benefits is MVC? You remember that *C* stands for a controller. Well, we will define one now. Create a `controller` package in the root package for the application and a member class `NoteController`:

```
package com.journaler.api.controller

import org.springframework.boot.autoconfigure.EnableAutoConfiguration
import org.springframework.http.MediaType
import org.springframework.web.bind.annotation.GetMapping
import org.springframework.web.bind.annotation.RequestMapping
import org.springframework.web.bind.annotation.RestController

@RestController
@RequestMapping("/notes")
@EnableAutoConfiguration
class NoteController {

    @GetMapping(
            value = "/obtain",
            produces = arrayOf(MediaType.APPLICATION_JSON_VALUE)
    )
    fun getNotes() : String {
        return "Work in progress."
```

```
        }
    }
```

Let's explain what is going on in this code. The `NoteController` class will be responsible for all operations related to `note` entities. The class itself has several very important annotations applied:

- `@RestController` is an annotation that is itself annotated with `@Controller` and `@ResponseBody`. The difference between a standard MVC controller (`@Controller`) and `@RestController` is in how the HTTP response body is created. `@Controller` is used with View technology (usually returning HTML as a result). `@RestController` returns an instance of a class that is serialized in an HTTP response as JSON or XML.
- `@RequestMapping("/notes")` is an annotation with which we map all requests, starting with `"notes/"`, to this class. We can map the whole path of an API call or map just methods, as in our case.
- `@GetMapping(value = "/obtain",produces = arrayOf(MediaType.APPLICATION_JSON_VALUE))`, we map GET HTTP method to `"obtain"` path. The result we expect is JSON. So the `getNotes()` method will be triggered each time the client triggers the GET method for the URL `http://host/notes/obtain`. We will, for now, just return a simple string.

What else is available?

We can map requests in several ways and support multiple methods with different media types (JSON, XML, and so on). For HTTP method mapping, Spring supports the following annotations:

- `@PostMapping` maps the POST method
- `@PutMapping` maps the PUT method
- `@DeleteMapping` maps the DELETE method, and so on

The same can be achieved like this:

```
@RequestMapping(
            method = arrayOf(RequestMethod.GET),
            value = "/obtain",
            produces = arrayOf(MediaType.APPLICATION_JSON_VALUE)
) fun getNotes(): String ...
```

 Note that we can assign multiple HTTP methods to request mapping!

Let's take a look at the parameters which annotations accept. Open the source code for the `@GetMapping` annotation. You will notice that actually, all parameters are explained in the `@RequestMapping` annotation. Follow it and open the class file. The following parameters can be passed to annotation:

- `name`: Assigning a name to mapping.
- `value`: Mapping we assign. This parameter can also accept multiple mappings, for example:

    ```
    value={"", "/something", "something*", "something/*,
    **/something"}
    ```

- `path`: Only in the Servlet environment, the path mapping URIs
- `method`: HTTP method to map `GET`, `POST`, `HEAD`, `OPTIONS`, `PUT`, `PATCH`, `DELETE`, and `TRACE`
- `params`: Parameters of the mapping
- `headers`: Headers of the mapping
- `consumes`: Consumable media types of the mapping
- `produces`: Producible media types of the mapping

Adding a data class

The `getNotes()` method, for now, returns just a string with the value `Work in progress`. This is not the list of notes we expect. To be able to return notes, we must define it. Create a new package called `data` with a `Note` member class. Make sure it is defined as follows:

```
package com.journaler.api.data
data class Note(
        var id: String = ,""
        var title: String,
        var message: String,
var location: String = ""
)
```

This is an ordinary Kotlin data class. We defined the `Note` class as the class with three mandatory fields and one optional field. Update `NoteController` so that it returns us two hardcoded notes:

```
@RestController
@RequestMapping("/notes")
class NoteController {

    @GetMapping(
            value = "/obtain",
            produces = arrayOf(MediaType.APPLICATION_JSON_VALUE)
    )
    fun getNotes(): List<Note> {
        return listOf(
                Note(
                        UUID.randomUUID().toString(),
                        "My first note",
                        "This is a message for the 1st note."
                ),
                Note(
                        UUID.randomUUID().toString(),
                        "My second note",
                        "This is a message for the 2nd note."
                )
        )
    }
}
```

Drafting other API calls

In the next chapter, we will obtain data from the database and return everything dynamically but, for now, we will be happy to have at least this dummy data. Let's apply all that we have learned so far to the rest of our API calls.

Define an entity for TODOs and create a `Todo` data class with the following fields:

```
package com.journaler.api.data

data class Todo(
        var id: String = "",
        var title: String,
        var message: String,
        var schedule: Long,
var location: String = ""
)
```

We are ready to write a controller class for TODOs. Before we do so, let's draft the rest of the `Note` entity API calls:

```
package com.journaler.api.controller

import com.journaler.api.data.Note
import org.springframework.http.MediaType
import org.springframework.web.bind.annotation.*
import java.util.*

@RestController
@RequestMapping("/notes")
class NoteController {

    /**
     * Get notes.
     */
    @GetMapping(
            value = "/obtain",
            produces = arrayOf(MediaType.APPLICATION_JSON_VALUE)
    )
    fun getNotes(): List<Note> {
        return listOf(
                Note(
                        UUID.randomUUID().toString(),
                        "My first note",
                        "This is a message for the 1st note."
```

```kotlin
            ),
            Note(
                    UUID.randomUUID().toString(),
                    "My second note",
                    "This is a message for the 2nd note."
            )
        )
}


/**
 * Insert note.
 * It consumes JSON, that is: request body Note.
 */
@PutMapping(
        value = "/insert",
        produces = arrayOf(MediaType.APPLICATION_JSON_VALUE),
        consumes = arrayOf(MediaType.APPLICATION_JSON_VALUE)
)
fun insertNote(
        @RequestBody note: Note
): Note {
    note.id = UUID.randomUUID().toString()
    return note
}


/**
 * Remove note by Id.
 * We introduced path variable for Id to pass.
 */
@DeleteMapping(
        value = "/delete/{id}",
        produces = arrayOf(MediaType.APPLICATION_JSON_VALUE)
)
fun deleteNote(@PathVariable(name = "id") id: String): Boolean {
    println("Removing: $id")
    return true
}

/**
 * Update item.
 * It consumes JSON, that is: request body Note.
 * As result it returns updated Note.
 */
@PostMapping(
        value = "/update",
        produces = arrayOf(MediaType.APPLICATION_JSON_VALUE),
        consumes = arrayOf(MediaType.APPLICATION_JSON_VALUE)
)
```

```
fun updateNote(@RequestBody note:Note): Note {
        note.title += " [ updated ]"
        note.message += " [ updated ]"
return note
}


}
```

For `Note`, we added the `INSERT`, `UPDATE`, and `DELETE` methods. As you can see here, we demonstrated how the `consumes` parameter is used. We also introduced the use of `@PathVariable`, so our call is parameterized through the path.

Now create `TodoController` in the same package as `NoteController`:

```
package com.journaler.api.controller

import com.journaler.api.data.Todo
import org.springframework.http.MediaType
import org.springframework.web.bind.annotation.*
import java.util.*

@RestController
@RequestMapping("/todos")
class TodoController {

    /**
     * Get todos.
     */
    @GetMapping(
            value = "/obtain",
            produces = arrayOf(MediaType.APPLICATION_JSON_VALUE)
    )
    fun getTodos(): List<Todo> {
        return listOf(
                Todo(
                        UUID.randomUUID().toString(),
                        "My first todo",
                        "This is a message for the 1st todo.",
                        System.currentTimeMillis()
                ),
                Todo(
                        UUID.randomUUID().toString(),
                        "My second todo",
                        "This is a message for the 2nd todo.",
                        System.currentTimeMillis()
                )
```

```kotlin
        )
    }

    /**
     * Insert item.
     * It consumes JSON, that is: request body Todo.
     */
    @PutMapping(
            value = "/insert",
            produces = arrayOf(MediaType.APPLICATION_JSON_VALUE),
            consumes = arrayOf(MediaType.APPLICATION_JSON_VALUE)
    )
    fun insertTodo(
            @RequestBody todo: Todo
    ): Todo {
        todo.id = UUID.randomUUID().toString()
        return todo
    }

    /**
     * Remove item by Id.
     * We introduced path variable for Id to pass.
     */
    @DeleteMapping(
            value = "/delete/{id}",
            produces = arrayOf(MediaType.APPLICATION_JSON_VALUE)
    )
    fun deleteTodo(@PathVariable(name = "id") id: String): Boolean {
        println("Removing: $id")
        return true
    }

    /**
     * Update item.
     * It consumes JSON, that is: request body Todo.
     * As result it returns updated Todo.
     */
    @PostMapping(
            value = "/update",
            produces = arrayOf(MediaType.APPLICATION_JSON_VALUE),
            consumes = arrayOf(MediaType.APPLICATION_JSON_VALUE)
    )
    fun updateTodo(@RequestBody todo: Todo): Todo {
        todo.title += " [ updated ]"
        todo.message += " [ updated ]"
        todo.schedule = System.currentTimeMillis()
        return todo
```

```
        }

    }
```

The implementation is practically the same, except that it handles the `Todo` entity and introduces one additional field.

 Update methods append a string to title and message. In our response, we can see that this is actually working. In practice, we will just update our data in the database without any modification on the data from payload to the server side.

Since we already know which operation to the performance based on the HTTP method, we will remove the `value` parameter from each HTTP method mapping except `DELETE`. `DELETE` HTTP mapping will keep the ID part:

- `NoteController`, responsible for `Note` entity-related things:

```
@RestController
@RequestMapping("/notes")
class NoteController {

    /**
     * Get notes.
     */
    @GetMapping(
            produces = arrayOf(MediaType.APPLICATION_JSON_VALUE)
    )
    fun getNotes(): List<Note> {
        return listOf(
                Note(
                        UUID.randomUUID().toString(),
                        "My first note",
                        "This is a message for the 1st note."
                ),
                Note(
                        UUID.randomUUID().toString(),
                        "My second note",
                        "This is a message for the 2nd note."
                )
        )
    }

    /**
     * Insert note.
     * It consumes JSON, that is: request body Note.
```

```
        */
    @PutMapping(
            produces = arrayOf(MediaType.APPLICATION_JSON_VALUE),
            consumes = arrayOf(MediaType.APPLICATION_JSON_VALUE)
    )
    fun insertNote(
            @RequestBody note: Note
    ): Note {
        note.id = UUID.randomUUID().toString()
        return note
    }

    /**
     * Remove note by Id.
     * We introduced path variable for Id to pass.
     */
    @DeleteMapping(
            value = "/{id}",
            produces = arrayOf(MediaType.APPLICATION_JSON_VALUE)
    )
    fun deleteNote(@PathVariable(name = "id") id: String): Boolean
{

        println("Removing: $id")
        return true
    }

    /**
     * Update item.
     * It consumes JSON, that is: request body Note.
     * As result it returns updated Note.
     */
    @PostMapping(
            produces = arrayOf(MediaType.APPLICATION_JSON_VALUE),
            consumes = arrayOf(MediaType.APPLICATION_JSON_VALUE)
    )
    fun updateNote(@RequestBody note: Note): Note {
        note.title += " [ updated ]"
        note.message += " [ updated ]"
        return note
    }

}
```

- TodoController, **responsible for** Todo **entity-related things:**

```
@RestController
@RequestMapping("/todos")
class TodoController {
```

```kotlin
/**
 * Get todos.
 */
@GetMapping(
        produces = arrayOf(MediaType.APPLICATION_JSON_VALUE)
)
fun getTodos(): List<Todo> {
    return listOf(
            Todo(
                    UUID.randomUUID().toString(),
                    "My first todo",
                    "This is a message for the 1st todo.",
                    System.currentTimeMillis()
            ),
            Todo(
                    UUID.randomUUID().toString(),
                    "My second todo",
                    "This is a message for the 2nd todo.",
                    System.currentTimeMillis()
            )
    )
}

/**
 * Insert item.
 * It consumes JSON, that is: request body Todo.
 */
@PutMapping(
        produces = arrayOf(MediaType.APPLICATION_JSON_VALUE),
        consumes = arrayOf(MediaType.APPLICATION_JSON_VALUE)
)
fun insertTodo(
        @RequestBody todo: Todo
): Todo {
    todo.id = UUID.randomUUID().toString()
    return todo
}

/**
 * Remove item by Id.
 * We introduced path variable for Id to pass.
 */
@DeleteMapping(
        value = "/{id}",
        produces = arrayOf(MediaType.APPLICATION_JSON_VALUE)
)
fun deleteTodo(@PathVariable(name = "id") id: String): Boolean
{
```

```
            println("Removing: $id")
            return true
    }

    /**
     * Update item.
     * It consumes JSON, that is: request body Todo.
     * As result it returns updated Todo.
     */
    @PostMapping(
            produces = arrayOf(MediaType.APPLICATION_JSON_VALUE),
            consumes = arrayOf(MediaType.APPLICATION_JSON_VALUE)
    )
    fun updateTodo(@RequestBody todo: Todo): Todo {
        todo.title += " [ updated ]"
        todo.message += " [ updated ]"
        todo.schedule = System.currentTimeMillis()
        return todo
    }

}
```

To sum up, we have just optimized our API definition in the preceding code and now we have the following API calls defined:

- For Notes:
  - [GET] /notes, to obtain a list of notes
  - [PUT] /notes, to insert a new Note
  - [DELETE] /notes/{id}, to remove an existing Note with ID
  - [POST] /notes, to update an existing Note
- For TODOs:
  - [GET] /todos, to obtain a list of TODOs
  - [PUT] /todos, to insert a new TODO
  - [DELETE] /todos/{id}, to remove an existing TODO with ID
  - [POST] /todos, to update an existing TODO

Our API is drafted and ready to run. In the next section, we will actually try each of our API calls using Postman, after we do a little configuring and start the application.

Running the application

Next, we need to run our application and trigger API methods. Add a file named `application.properties` to your application resources folder:

```
spring.application.name= Journaler API
server.port= 9000
```

This will represent the configuration of our local development environment. Thanks to Spring Boot, it is possible to externalize configuration so we can work with the same application code in different environments.

So, what have we done in these three lines?

- `spring.application.name`: We assigned the application name
- `server.port`: We assigned the port on which our application will start and listen

What else can be configured? First of all, we can configure logging. Let's extend our `application.properties`:

```
...
logging.level.root=INFO
logging.level.com.journaler.api=DEBUG
logging.level.org.springframework.jdbc=ERROR
```

The following log levels are supported:

- TRACE
- DEBUG
- INFO
- WARN
- ERROR
- FATAL
- OFF

Spring Boot uses commons-logging (https://commons.apache.org/proper/commons-logging/) for all logging performed internally. Spring log implementation is not closed, so it's possible to extend it.

Besides logging, frequently configured environment-related parameters can be the following:

- Defining custom values
- Access to the data source
- Defining keys (for example, `apple.api.key= ...`)
- Overriding server-specific parameters (for example, `spring.http.multipart.max-file-size= ...`) and many more!

Run the application and wait until it starts. After a couple of seconds, the application will be up and running:

```
2018-05-11 11:57:10.874  INFO 3340 --- [           main] o.s.j.e.a.AnnotationMBeanExporter         : Registering beans for JMX exposure on startup
2018-05-11 11:57:11.638  INFO 3340 --- [           main] o.s.b.w.embedded.tomcat.TomcatWebServer  : Tomcat started on port(s): 9000 (http)
2018-05-11 11:57:11.663  INFO 3340 --- [           main] com.journaler.api.ApiApplicationKt       : Started ApiApplicationKt in 21.007 seconds (JVM running
 for 26.738)
```

Observe the startup log. What do you see? Take a look at each line closely. You can see the whole lifecycle of our application:

- Starting with `ApiApplication.Kt` on `YOUR_HOST.local` with `PID...` (started by `YOUR_USERNAME...`), the application start sequence is initialized
- Running with Spring Boot v2.0.0.M4, Spring v5.0.0.RC4, the application will use Spring 5 with Spring Boot version 2
- Tomcat initialized with the port: `9000` (HTTP), we will use Tomcat to serve the content running on the port we defined in our `application.properties` configuration

Then, a little further on, all the request mappings we defined will appear. Let's take a look at the first mapping log:

```
Mapped "{[/notes],methods=[GET],produces=[application/json]}"
onto public java.util.List<com.journaler.api.data.Note>
com.journaler.api.controller.NoteController.getNotes()
```

This can be very useful if some of your mappings don't work, or if you want to check whether something is mapped at all. The good thing is that we see all the mappings the application has! This is especially convenient if you are observing the start log for the application that you are extending, but it has been developed by somebody else.

Finally, we see these lines:

```
Tomcat started on port(s): 9000 (http)
Started ApiApplicationKt in 11.369 seconds
```

Now we can trigger API calls! Open Postman and try it out!

In the following, we will be trying notes API that calls. Let's take a couple of minutes to try API calls:

- [**GET**] `http://localhost:9000/notes`:

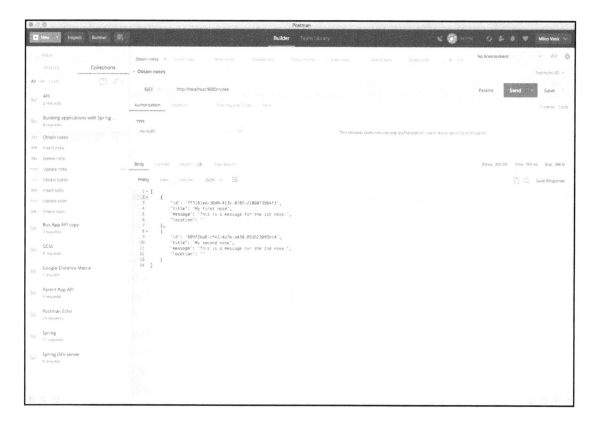

- [**PUT**] `http://localhost:9000/notes:`

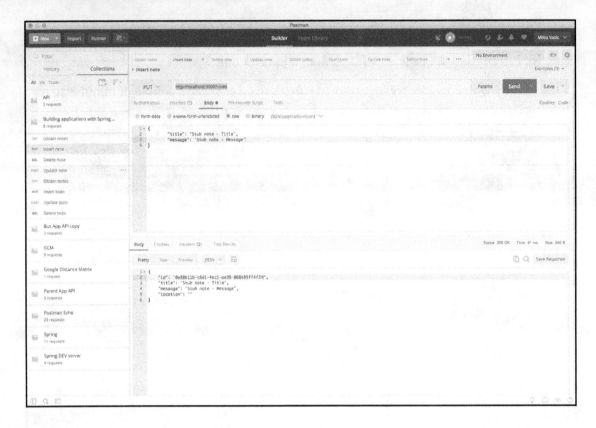

- [**DELETE**
  ]`http://localhost:9000/notes/f79464fc-21d6-4b3a-8871-6c5e853d73`
  `45`:

- [**POST**] `http://localhost:9000/notes`:

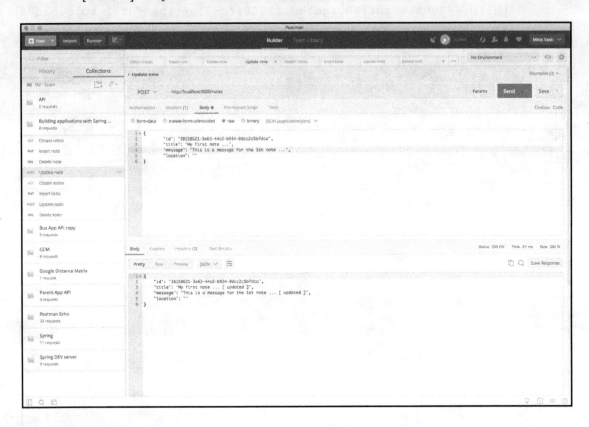

In the following, we will be trying TODOs API calls.

- [**GET**] http://localhost:9000/todos:

- **[PUT]** `http://localhost:9000/todos:`

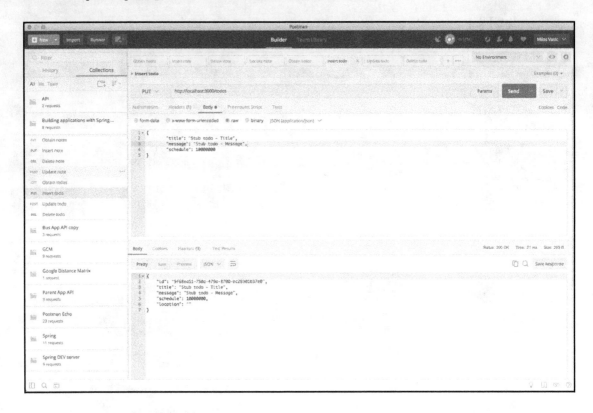

- [**POST**] `http://localhost:9000/todos:`

- [**DELETE**
  ] `http://localhost:9000/todos/38158621-3e63-44c2-b934-0dcc2c5b7d`
  `ca:`

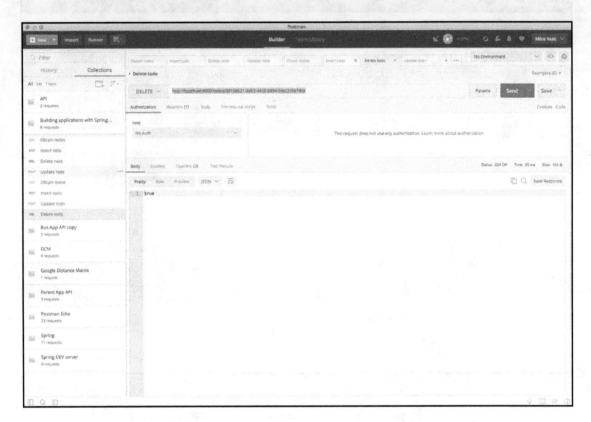

Accessing Actuator endpoints

Let's check out some endpoints that come with Actuator out of the box:

- `/application/health`: Application health
- `/application/info`: Application information
- `/application/metrics`: Metrics information for the application running
- `/application/trace`: Trace information for the last few HTTP requests

This is not a complete list. This is a list of the most commonly used Actuator endpoints. Since data we access can be *sensitive*, not all endpoints are enabled by default. To enable all these calls, open your `application.properties` and update it:

```
endpoints.health.enabled=true
endpoints.trace.enabled=true
endpoints.info.enabled=true
endpoints.metrics.enabled=true
```

Start the application and try Actuator endpoints one by one. You should get responses similar to these:

- [**GET**] `http://localhost:9000/application/status`:

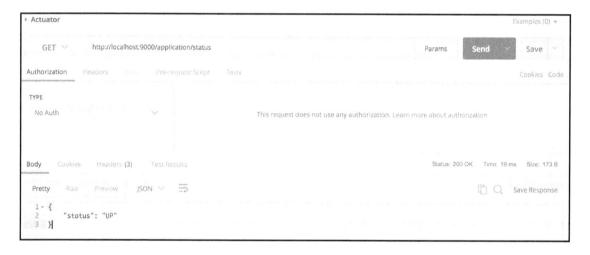

- **[GET]** `http://localhost:9000/application/health:`

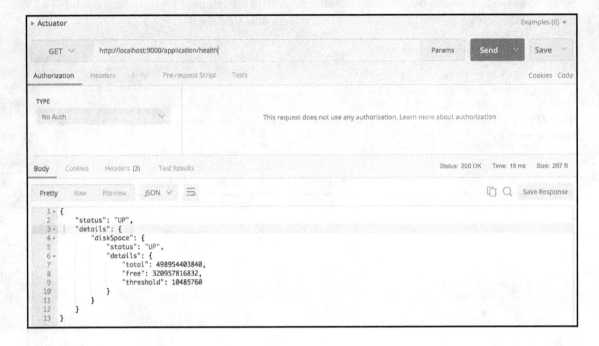

- [**GET**] http://localhost:9000/application/metrics:

- [**GET**] `http://localhost:9000/application/trace:`

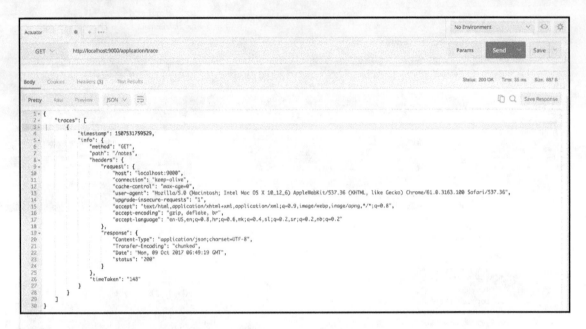

Adding an @Service component

We will continue our work by introducing a `Service` component. So, what is a Spring service exactly? An `@Service` annotated class is `Service`, originally defined by domain-driven design. That is *an operation offered as an interface that stands alone in the model, with no encapsulated state.*

Spring offers the following commonly used annotations:

- `@Component`
- `@Controller`
- `@Repository`
- `@Service`

Let's explain the difference between them.

- @Component is a generalization stereotype for any component managed by Spring Framework.

The following specializations are available: @Repository, @Service, and @Controller. Each is specialized for a different use:

- @Repository annotation is a marker for any class that fulfills the role of a **Data Access Object (DAO)** of a repository. It also offers the automatic translation of exceptions. We will explain its usage soon.
- @Controller annotation has already been covered in the previous examples.
- @Service annotated class will have the purpose of connecting a controller with all operations to all operations related to data repository.

Any class annotated with @Controller, @Repository, or @Service is actually annotated with @Component too.

The following implementation will demonstrate the use of the @Service component. Create a service package in the root package of your project and two member classes: NoteService and TodoService. We will start with NoteService:

```
package com.journaler.api.service

import com.journaler.api.data.Note
import org.springframework.stereotype.Service
import java.util.*

@Service("Note service")
class NoteService {

    fun getNotes(): List<Note> = listOf(
            Note(
                    UUID.randomUUID().toString(),
                    "My first note",
                    "This is a message for the 1st note."
            ),
            Note(
                    UUID.randomUUID().toString(),
                    "My second note",
                    "This is a message for the 2nd note."
            )
```

```kotlin
    )

    fun insertNote(note: Note): Note {
        note.id = UUID.randomUUID().toString()
        return note
    }

    fun deleteNote(id: String): Boolean = false

    fun updateNote(note: Note): Boolean = true

}
```

The class is annotated with `@Service` annotation and a name assigned. The implementation will actually represent the CRUD operation we plan to perform. For now, we will keep *dummy* implementations. In the next chapter, we will connect these methods with the `Repository` component.

We defined `Service` components. Now we have to change our controller class:

```kotlin
@RestController
@RequestMapping("/notes")
class NoteController {

    @Autowired
    private lateinit var service: NoteService

    /**
     * Get notes.
     */
    @GetMapping(
            produces = arrayOf(MediaType.APPLICATION_JSON_VALUE)
    )
    fun getNotes() = service.getNotes()

    /**
     * Insert note.
     * It consumes JSON, that is: request body Note.
     */
    @PutMapping(
            produces = arrayOf(MediaType.APPLICATION_JSON_VALUE),
            consumes = arrayOf(MediaType.APPLICATION_JSON_VALUE)
    )
    fun insertNote(
            @RequestBody note: Note
    ) = service.insertNote(note)
```

```
/**
 * Remove note by Id.
 * We introduced path variable for Id to pass.
 */
@DeleteMapping(
        value = "/{id}",
        produces = arrayOf(MediaType.APPLICATION_JSON_VALUE)
)
fun deleteNote(
        @PathVariable(name = "id") id: String
): Boolean = service.deleteNote(id)

/**
 * Update item.
 * It consumes JSON, that is: request body Note.
 * As result it returns boolean, True == success.
 */
@PostMapping(
        produces = arrayOf(MediaType.APPLICATION_JSON_VALUE),
        consumes = arrayOf(MediaType.APPLICATION_JSON_VALUE)
)
fun updateNote(
        @RequestBody note: Note
): Boolean = service.updateNote(note)


}
```

The controller performs the same functionality, except that implementation is moved to a `Service` component. The most significant new thing is the `@Autowired` annotation. With `@Autowired`, we tell Spring Framework that a particular field must be dependency injected. The field must be defined as late init `var`.

Let's do the same for TODOs. Make sure `TodoService` looks like this:

```
package com.journaler.api.service

import com.journaler.api.data.Todo
import org.springframework.stereotype.Service
import java.util.*


@Service("Todo service")
class TodoService {

    fun getTodos(): List<Todo> = listOf(
            Todo(
                    UUID.randomUUID().toString(),
```

```
                            "My first todo",
                            "This is a message for the 1st todo.",
                            System.currentTimeMillis()
                    ),
                    Todo(
                            UUID.randomUUID().toString(),
                            "My second todo",
                            "This is a message for the 2nd todo.",
                            System.currentTimeMillis()
                    )
            )

    fun insertTodo(todo: Todo): Todo {
        todo.id = UUID.randomUUID().toString()
        return todo
    }

    fun deleteTodo(id: String): Boolean = false

    fun updateTodo(todo: Todo): Boolean = true

}
```

TodoController now looks like this and it is using injected TodoService:

```
@RestController
@RequestMapping("/todos")
class TodoController {

    @Autowired
    private lateinit var service: TodoService

    /**
     * Get todos.
     */
    @GetMapping(
            produces = arrayOf(MediaType.APPLICATION_JSON_VALUE)
    )
    fun getTodos(): List<Todo> = service.getTodos()

    /**
     * Insert item.
     * It consumes JSON, that is: request body Todo.
     */
    @PutMapping(
            produces = arrayOf(MediaType.APPLICATION_JSON_VALUE),
            consumes = arrayOf(MediaType.APPLICATION_JSON_VALUE)
    )
    fun insertTodo(
```

```
        @RequestBody todo: Todo
): Todo = service.insertTodo(todo)

/**
 * Remove item by Id.
 * We introduced path variable for Id to pass.
 */
@DeleteMapping(
        value = "/{id}",
        produces = arrayOf(MediaType.APPLICATION_JSON_VALUE)
)
fun deleteTodo(
        @PathVariable(name = "id") id: String
): Boolean = service.deleteTodo(id)

/**
 * Update item.
 * It consumes JSON, that is: request body Todo.
 * As result it returns boolean. True == success.
 */
@PostMapping(
        produces = arrayOf(MediaType.APPLICATION_JSON_VALUE),
        consumes = arrayOf(MediaType.APPLICATION_JSON_VALUE)
)
fun updateTodo(@RequestBody todo: Todo): Boolean =
service.updateTodo(todo)

}
```

See, simple! It was very easy to extract this code and delegate it to a `Service` component.

Summary

In this chapter, we defined our first API call and drafted the others. We covered everything that is needed to specify your RESTful application. We also separated requested related stuff from domain-related implementations by introducing Service. In the next chapter, we will replace *dummy data* and *dummy implementation* with real data access and introduce repositories.

Working with Spring Data JPA and MySQL

In this chapter, we will continue our journey toward working with data in Spring. As you already know, the API we defined does not persist or read from any real data source. We will take care of this by demonstrating Spring's powerful data features. We will use Spring Data JPA and MySQL as our database.

In this chapter, we will cover the following topics:

- Introducing Spring Data JPA
- Installing MySQL
- CRUD operations
- Creating database queries

Introducing Spring Data JPA

Spring Data JPA is a part of Spring Data. Spring Data is much bigger than Spring Data JPA, so we will start by explaining it. Spring Data, as Spring-based programming, provides us with mechanisms for misc underlying data storage.

Thanks to Spring Data, we can utilize different data storage options. We can access different relational or non-relational databases. In this book, we will be focusing on a MySQL database.As a parent, Spring contains multiple sub-projects; one of them is Spring Data JPA.

What does Spring Data provide?

Let's highlight some of the most important features that Spring Data provides:

- Repository and custom object-mapping abstractions
- Derivation of dynamic queries from the repository method names
- Auditing
- Custom repositories
- Ease of integration and configuration
- Ease of use with Spring MVC controllers

Which Spring Data modules do we need?

For us, the most important modules are the following:

- Spring Data Commons, core components for Spring Data
- Spring Data JPA, components for the implementation of JPA repositories

About Spring Data JPA

As we said, Spring Data JPA contains components for implementing JPA repositories. Thanks to Spring Data JPA, it's easy to create applications that use data access technologies.

Spring Data JPA provides the following set of features:

- Support for creating repositories based on Spring and JPA
- Support for Querydsl (http://www.querydsl.com/) predicates
- Auditing
- Pagination support
- Support for dynamic query execution
- Support for custom data access implementation
- @Query annotated queries validation performed at Bootstrap time
- @EnableJpaRepositories annotation to configure JavaConfig-based repositories

Installing MySQL

As we will be focusing on a MySQL database as our storage, you have to install it on your system if you don't already have it installed. For our purposes, MySQL Community Server will do the job. Go to `https://dev.mysql.com/downloads/mysql/` and download the installation for your operating system:

Perform the installation procedure for your operating system:

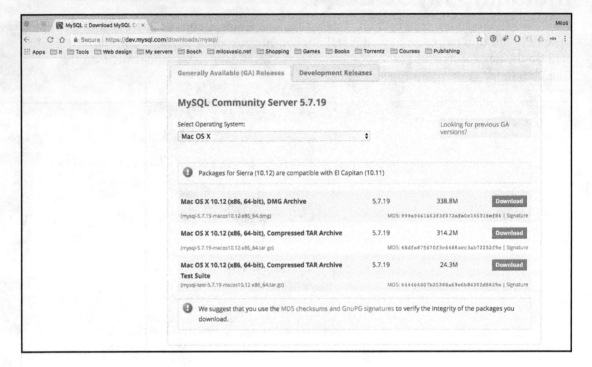

Installing MySQL Community Server on macOS

For macOS, MySQL is available in two variants:

- DMG with the installation wizard
- TAR archive—we must extract its content before installation

We will use the DMG option as the preferred one. Open the DMG file and launch the installation package:

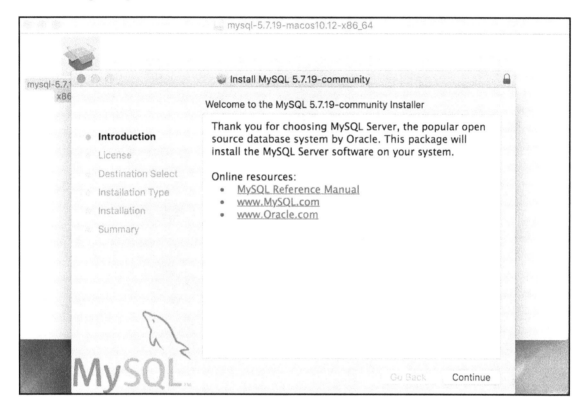

Follow the installation instructions. After the installation is complete, you will get root credentials for your MySQL instance:

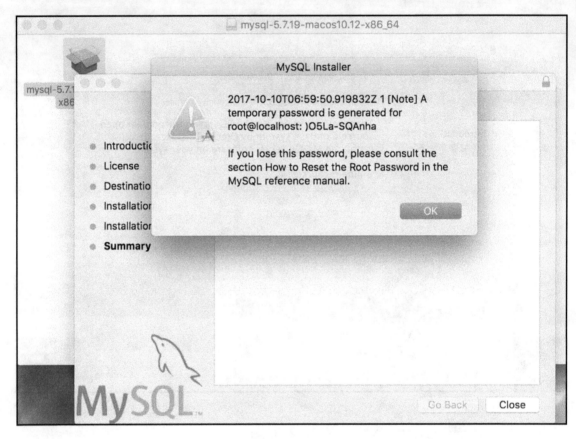

Confirm by clicking on **OK**. Close the installer and eject the DMG image.

Now open **System Preference** | **MySQL**:

You will see your local instance status. If it is not running, start it:

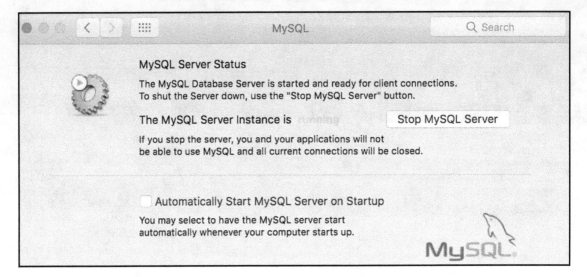

We choose not to start MySQL with system startup. That is your decision.

Installing MySQL Community Server on Windows

Before you start with the installation, make sure you have Microsoft Visual C++ 2013 Redistributable Package installed. If you don't have it, please install it from the Microsoft Download Center.

Run the setup. Choose the setup type for your operating system. We recommend you use **Developer Default**. Follow the installation instructions that provides you the wizard. MySQL will be installed and started.

Installing MySQL Community Server on Linux

We will focus on installation using Generic Binaries. We can obtain it by downloading the compressed TAR or by installing it with the system's software package manager.

Using a software package manager

We will cover the most commonly used software package managers. Let's start with YUM (DNF). Start Terminal and run the commands as a privileged user.

For Installing MySQL using YUM:

- Fedora 26:

  ```
  $ dnf install
  https://dev.mysql.com/get/mysql57-community-release-fc26-10.noarch.
  rpm
  ```

- Fedora 25:

  ```
  $ dnf install
  https://dev.mysql.com/get/mysql57-community-release-fc25-10.noarch.
  rpm
  ```

- Fedora 24:

  ```
  $ dnf install
  https://dev.mysql.com/get/mysql57-community-release-fc24-10.noarch.
  rpm
  ```

- CentOS 7 and Red Hat Enterprise Linux 7:

  ```
  $ yum localinstall
  https://dev.mysql.com/get/mysql57-community-release-el7-11.noarch.r
  pm
  ```

- CentOS 6 and Red Hat Enterprise Linux 6:

  ```
  $ yum localinstall
  https://dev.mysql.com/get/mysql57-community-release-el6-11.noarch.r
  pm
  ```

For Installing MySQL using DNF:

- Fedora 26, 25, 24:

  ```
  $ dnf install mysql-community-server
  ```

- CentOS 7, 6, and Red Hat Enterprise Linux 7, 6:

  ```
  $ yum install mysql-community-server
  ```

When the installation is complete, start a MySQL server local instance and enable autostart:

- Fedora 26, 25, 24, CentOS 7, and Red Hat Enterprise Linux 7:

```
$ systemctl start mysqld.service
$ systemctl enable mysqld.service
```

- CentOS 6 and Red Hat Enterprise Linux 6:

```
$ service mysql start
$ chkconfig --levels 235 mysqld on
```

This step is very important! Obtain your root password:

```
$ grep 'A temporary password is generated for root@localhost'
/var/log/mysqld.log | tail -1
```

You should get something like this:

```
... A temporary password is generated for root@localhost: )O5La-SQAnha
```

Using TAR

Extract the TAR content at the `/usr/local/mysql` location.

Then follow the procedure:

```
$ groupadd mysql
$ useradd -r -g mysql -s /bin/false mysql
$ cd /usr/local
$ tar zxvf [ path to your downloaded file  ].tar.gz
$ ln -s [ full path to mysql] mysql
$ cd mysql
$ mkdir mysql-files
$ chmod 750 mysql-files
$ chown -R mysql .
$ chgrp -R mysql .
$ bin/mysql_install_db -user=mysql
$ bin/mysqld --initialize --user=mysql
$ bin/mysql_ssl_rsa_setup
$ chown -R root .
$ chown -R mysql data mysql-files
$ bin/mysqld_safe --user=mysql &
$ cp support-files/mysql.server /etc/init.d/mysql.server
```

We have a MySQL local server instance up and running. We are ready to do some Spring Data JPA development!

Creating a schema

We need a schema that we will use for our application. Create a schema called `journaler_api` with default UTF-8 collation. For this purpose, it is up to you how you will access the local MySQL server instance and create a schema. We will use MySQL Workbench, as shown in the following screenshot:

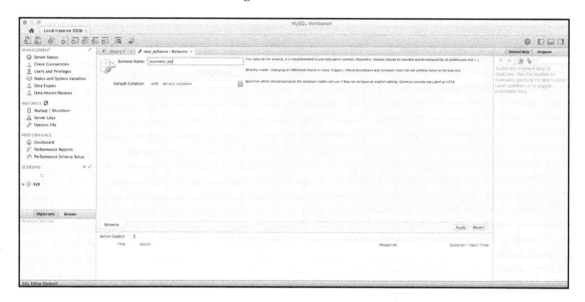

Review the SQL script, as shown in the following screenshot:

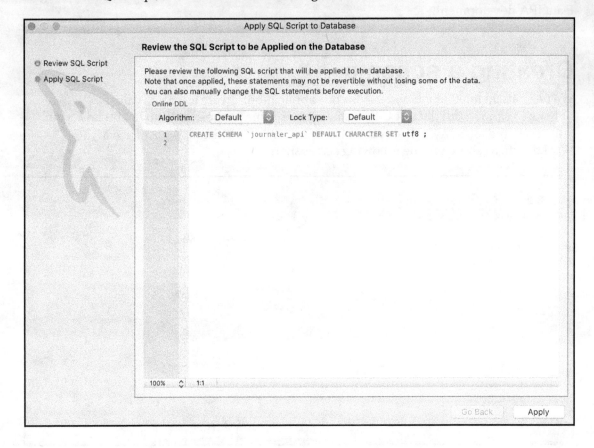

Apply the SQL script, as shown in the following screenshot:

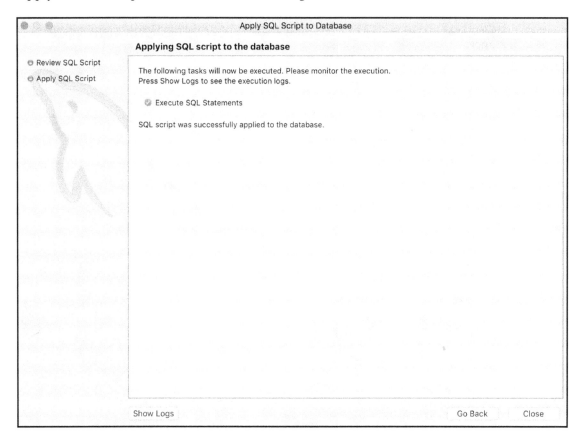

Extending dependencies

To work with Spring Data JPA, open your `build.gradle` and extend it:

```
...
dependencies {
    ...
    runtime('mysql:mysql-connector-java')
    compile("org.springframework.boot:spring-boot-starter-data-jpa")
    ...
}
```

We have provided the necessary dependencies and we have also added support for MySQL connector and Spring Data JPA. Next, what we need to do is to define our data source. Open the `application.properties` file and add configuration according to your local MySQL instance:

```
spring.datasource.url=jdbc:mysql://localhost/journaler_api?useSSL=false&use
Unicode=true&characterEncoding=utf-8
spring.datasource.username=root
spring.datasource.password=YOUR_MYSQL_ROOT_PASSWORD
spring.datasource.tomcat.test-on-borrow=true
spring.datasource.tomcat.validation-interval=30000
spring.datasource.tomcat.validation-query=SELECT 1
spring.datasource.tomcat.remove-abandoned=true
spring.datasource.tomcat.remove-abandoned-timeout=10000
spring.datasource.tomcat.log-abandoned=true
spring.datasource.tomcat.max-age=1800000
spring.datasource.tomcat.log-validation-errors=true
spring.datasource.tomcat.max-active=50
spring.datasource.tomcat.max-idle=10
spring.jpa.hibernate.ddl-auto=update
```

The explanation for the preceding code is as follows:

- The first line represents the path to the database:

  ```
  spring.datasource.url= ...
  ```

- Then we set the username and password that we will use to access the database:

  ```
  spring.datasource.username=root
  spring.datasource.password=YOUR_MYSQL_ROOT_PASSWORD
  ```

- Validate the connection before borrowing it from the pool:

  ```
  spring.datasource.tomcat.test-on-borrow=true
  ```

- Connection validation interval:

  ```
  spring.datasource.tomcat.validation-interval=30000
  ```

- Query used to validate connections from the pool before returning them to the caller:

  ```
  spring.datasource.tomcat.validation-query=SELECT 1
  ```

- Flag to remove abandoned connections if they exceed the remove abandoned timeout:

  ```
  spring.datasource.tomcat.remove-abandoned=true
  spring.datasource.tomcat.remove-abandoned-timeout=10000
  ```

- Log the stack trace of abandoned connections:

  ```
  spring.datasource.tomcat.log-abandoned=true
  ```

- Time in milliseconds to keep this connection:

  ```
  spring.datasource.tomcat.max-age=1800000
  ```

- Log validation errors:

  ```
  spring.datasource.tomcat.log-validation-errors=true
  ```

- A maximum number of active connections that can be allocated from the pool at the same time:

  ```
  spring.datasource.tomcat.max-active=50
  ```

- A maximum number of idle connections that should be kept in the pool:

  ```
  spring.datasource.tomcat.max-idle=10
  ```

- And finally, initialize the database using Hibernate:

  ```
  spring.jpa.hibernate.ddl-auto=update
  ```

Build and run the application. If you have provided a good URL and correct credentials, there will be no problems; the application will start. If anything goes wrong, thanks to this configuration, you will be able to see the stack trace.

Once the application is started, check whether the tables appear in the `journaler_api` database:

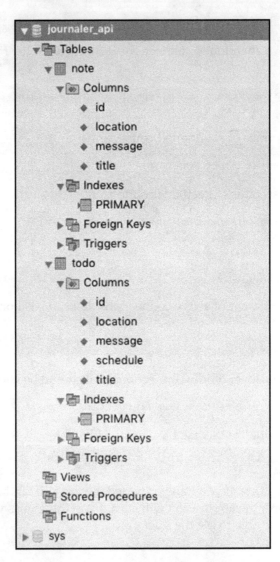

CRUD operations

To be able to perform CRUD operations with our data, we have to implement some code. We will make the necessary changes and introduce some new classes. What we will present to you now is a standard for every Spring application that manipulates the data stored in the relational database.

Create a package named `repository` with the `NoteRepository` interfaces as follows:

```
package com.journaler.api.repository

import com.journaler.api.data.Note
import org.springframework.data.repository.CrudRepository

/**
 * String is the type for ID we use.
 */
interface NoteRepository : CrudRepository<Note, String>

TodoRepository:
package com.journaler.api.repository

import com.journaler.api.data.Todo
import org.springframework.data.repository.CrudRepository

/**
 * String is the type for ID we use.
 */
interface TodoRepository : CrudRepository<Todo, String>
```

Both interfaces inherit `CrudRepository`. `CrudRepository` brings us the following functionalities:

- `save()`: Saving one entity
- `saveAll()`: Saving multiple entities
- `findById()`: Returns entity with ID
- `existsById()`: Does entity with ID exist
- `findAll()`: Returns all entities
- `findAllById()`: Returns all entities with ID
- `count()`: Returns the number of entities available

- `deleteById()`: Deletes entities with ID
- `delete()`: Deletes one entity
- `deleteAll()`: Deletes all entities received as argument
- `deleteAll()` (without arguments): Deletes all entities

Now, when we have repositories defined, we have to update our entities:

- Code for `Note`:

```
package com.journaler.api.data

import org.hibernate.annotations.GenericGenerator
import javax.persistence.*

@Entity
@Table(name = "note")
data class Note(
        @Id
        @GeneratedValue(generator = "uuid2")
        @GenericGenerator(name = "uuid2", strategy = "uuid2")
        @Column(columnDefinition = "varchar(36)")
        var id: String = "",
        var title: String,
        var message: String,
        var location: String = ""
) {

    /**
     * Hibernate tries creates a bean via reflection.
     * It does the object creation by calling the no-arg
constructor.
     * Then it uses the setter methods to set the properties.
     *
     * If there is no default constructor, the following excpetion
happens:
     * org.hibernate.InstantiationException: No default constructor
for entity...
     */
    constructor() : this(
            "", "", "", ""
    )

}
```

To use a class as a database entity, use @Entity annotation. To assign a table name to be used, use @Table annotation, as in our Note class example. @Id annotation is used to telling Spring what field our ID will be. As you can see, we are using UUID2 as ID for our data.

- Code for Todo:

```
package com.journaler.api.data

import org.hibernate.annotations.GenericGenerator
import javax.persistence.*

@Entity
@Table(name = "todo")
data class Todo(
        @Id
        @GeneratedValue(generator = "uuid2")
        @GenericGenerator(name = "uuid2", strategy = "uuid2")
        @Column(columnDefinition = "varchar(36)")
        var id: String = "",
        var title: String,
        var message: String,
        var schedule: Long,
        var location: String = ""
) {

    /**
     * Hibernate tries creates a bean via reflection.
     * It does the object creation by calling the no-arg
constructor.
     * Then it uses the setter methods to set the properties.
     *
     * If there is no default constructor, the following excpetion
happens:
     * org.hibernate.InstantiationException: No default constructor
for entity...
     */
    constructor() : this(
            "", "", "", -1, ""
    )

}
```

The way in which we defined the `Todo` class now is the same as the one that defined the `Note` class. We defined a repository for both entities and updated the entities themselves. We will continue with the changes and introduce repositories in our services. Update both services to use repositories, as we did in the following example:

- Code for `NoteService`:

```
package com.journaler.api.service

import com.journaler.api.data.Note
import com.journaler.api.repository.NoteRepository
import org.springframework.beans.factory.annotation.Autowired
import org.springframework.stereotype.Service

@Service("Note service")
class NoteService {

    @Autowired
    lateinit var repository: NoteRepository

    /**
     * Returns all instances of the type.
     *
     * @return all entities
     */
    fun getNotes(): Iterable<Note> = repository.findAll()

    /**
     * Saves a given entity. Use the returned instance for further
operations as
     * the save operation might have changed the entity instance
completely.
     *
     * @param entity must not be {@literal null}.
     * @return the saved entity will never be {@literal null}.
     */
    fun insertNote(note: Note): Note = repository.save(note)

    /**
     * Deletes the entity with the given id.
     *
     * @param id must not be {@literal null}.
     * @throws IllegalArgumentException in case the given {@code
id} is {@literal null}
     */
    fun deleteNote(id: String) = repository.deleteById(id)
```

```
/**
 * Saves a given entity. Use the returned instance for further
operations as
 * the save operation might have changed the entity instance
completely.
 *
 * @param entity must not be {@literal null}.
 * @return the saved entity will never be {@literal null}.
 */
fun updateNote(note: Note): Note = repository.save(note)

}
```

- Code for `TodoService`:

```
package com.journaler.api.service

import com.journaler.api.data.Todo
import com.journaler.api.repository.TodoRepository
import org.springframework.beans.factory.annotation.Autowired
import org.springframework.stereotype.Service


@Service("Todo service")
class TodoService {

    @Autowired
    lateinit var repository: TodoRepository

    fun getTodos(): Iterable<Todo> = repository.findAll()

    fun insertTodo(todo: Todo): Todo = repository.save(todo)

    fun deleteTodo(id: String) = repository.deleteById(id)

    fun updateTodo(todo: Todo): Todo = repository.save(todo)

}
```

The `Todo` service is implemented in exactly the same way as `Note` service, except that it doesn't have any documented code so it is easier for you to read. We updated our methods to use repository provided features. This means that this will affect our controllers too:

- Code for `NoteController`:

```
@RestController
@RequestMapping("/notes")
```

```
class NoteController {
    ...
    @DeleteMapping(
            value = "/{id}",
            produces = arrayOf(MediaType.APPLICATION_JSON_VALUE)
    )
    fun deleteNote(
            @PathVariable(name = "id") id: String
    ) = service.deleteNote(id)
    ...
    @PostMapping(
            produces = arrayOf(MediaType.APPLICATION_JSON_VALUE),
            consumes = arrayOf(MediaType.APPLICATION_JSON_VALUE)
    )
    fun updateNote(
            @RequestBody note: Note
    ) : Note = service.updateNote(note)
    ...
}
```

* Code for `TodoController`:

```
@RestController
@RequestMapping("/todos")
class TodoController {
    ...
    @GetMapping(
            produces = arrayOf(MediaType.APPLICATION_JSON_VALUE)
    )
    fun getTodos(): Iterable<Todo> = service.getTodos()
    ...
    @DeleteMapping(
            value = "/{id}",
            produces = arrayOf(MediaType.APPLICATION_JSON_VALUE)
    )
    fun deleteTodo(
            @PathVariable(name = "id") id: String
    ) = service.deleteTodo(id)
    ...
    @PostMapping(
            produces = arrayOf(MediaType.APPLICATION_JSON_VALUE),
            consumes = arrayOf(MediaType.APPLICATION_JSON_VALUE)
    )
    fun updateTodo(@RequestBody todo: Todo): Todo =
service.updateTodo(todo)
    ...
}
```

Let's try our application. Build it and start it. We will check each CRUD operation. Observe the changes in the payload introduced in the latest changes.

Insert

We will first apply **Insert note**:

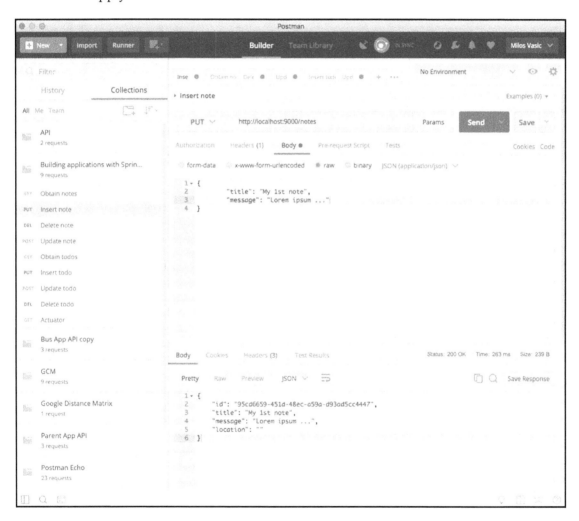

Execute an API call and insert several more Notes. It is up to you what the title and the content of the message will be.

Do the same for TODOs version of the API call:

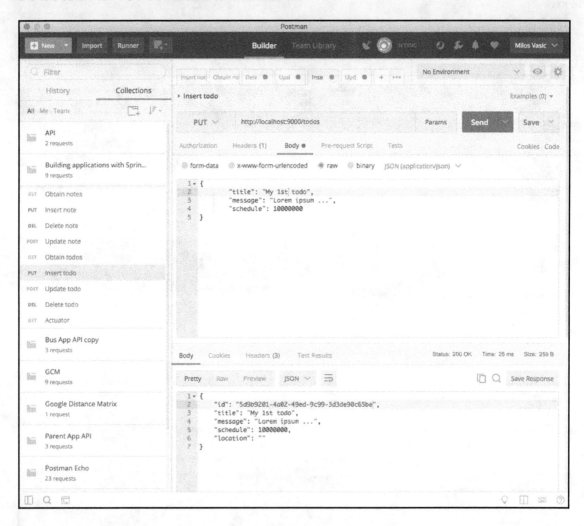

Create several TODOs.

Update

Write down IDs for one Note and for one of the TODOs you just created. Then, try to update the API call for each of them. Updating a Note will return the following result:

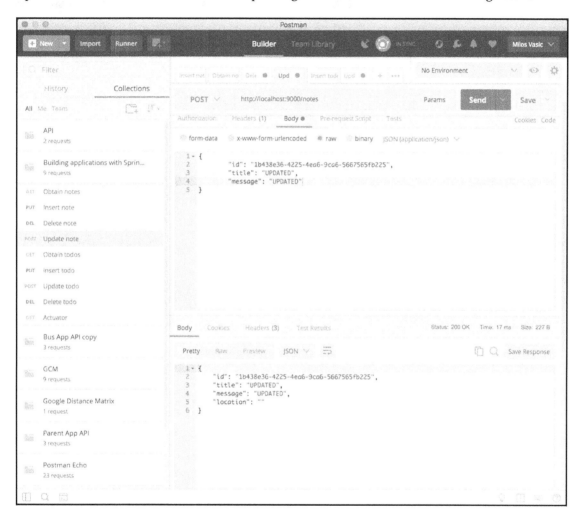

While updating, TODOs will return the following result:

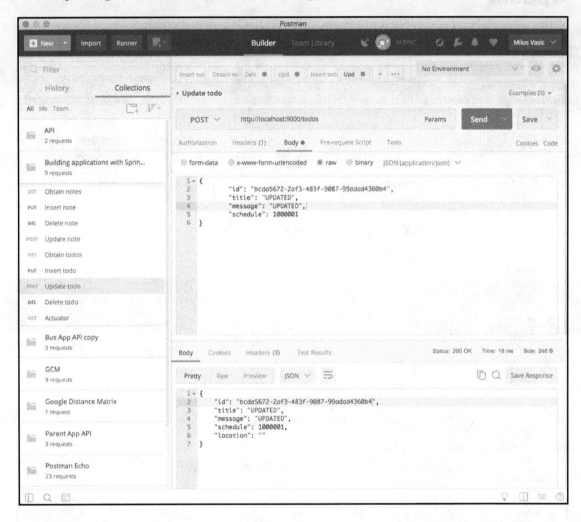

Select

Let's see what we have now in our database. Start by executing an obtain API call for Notes:

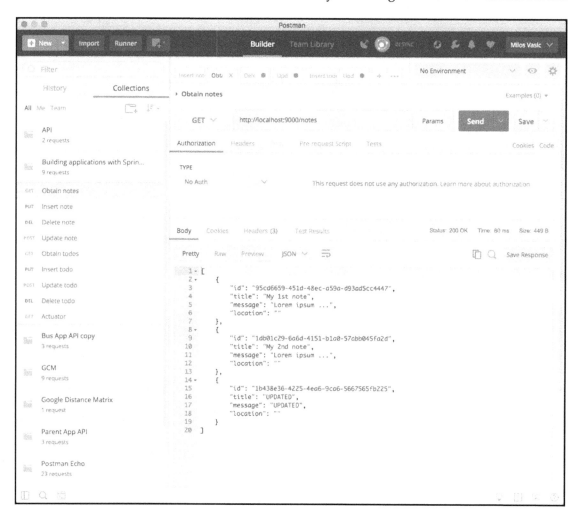

And do the same for TODOs:

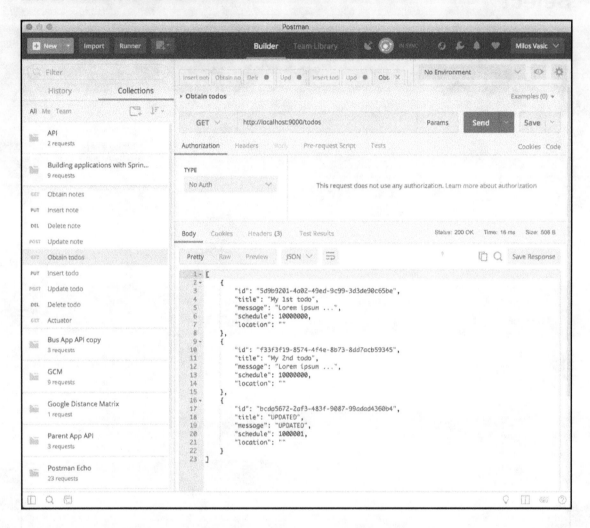

As you can see, all the items we inserted are there, including the updated ones.

Delete

Pick the IDs you want to delete and execute API calls for the removal of Note and TODOs.

Delete one Note first:

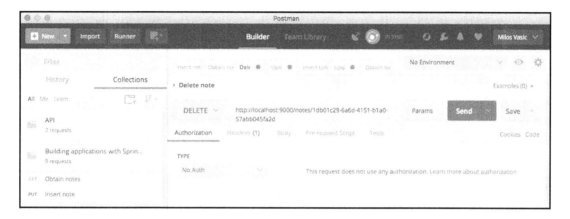

Then delete the TODOs:

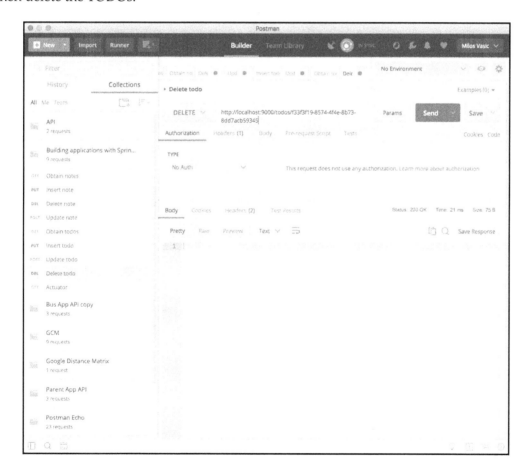

If you execute obtain API calls, you will see that the deleted items are missing.

More regarding updates

Let's try to update the API call one more time. Pick the Note you want to update. This time, set a new title only for the Note but leave out the message field. If you try to update, you will get an error:

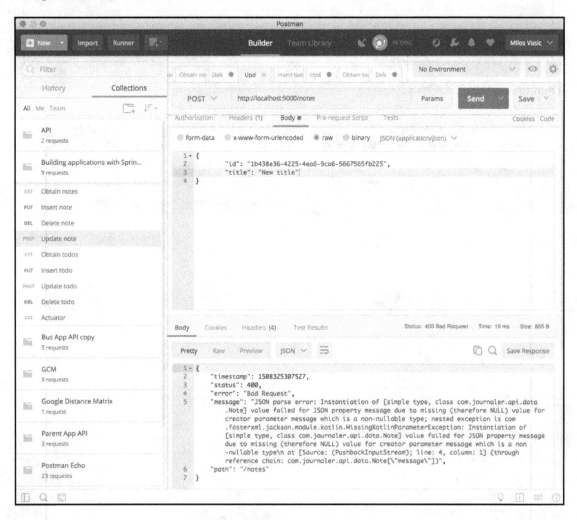

We have a problem! Let's fix it! To perform a successful update, you must provide the whole entity! All fields that were not provided in the payload to update the API call, but that are defined with the default values, will overwrite original values in our database! Use the whole payload you get from API calls. Do not trigger an update with manually populated instances!

Introducing DTOs

So far, we haven't created any **data transfer objects** (DTOs). It is time to do so. We will introduce two more fields. Extend the `Note` and `Todo` classes. Add created and modified fields:

- `Note`:

```
package com.journaler.api.data

import com.fasterxml.jackson.annotation.JsonInclude
import org.hibernate.annotations.CreationTimestamp
import org.hibernate.annotations.GenericGenerator
import org.hibernate.annotations.UpdateTimestamp
import java.util.*
import javax.persistence.*

@Entity
@Table(name = "note")
@JsonInclude(JsonInclude.Include.NON_NULL)
data class Note(
        ...
        @CreationTimestamp
        var created: Date = Date(),
        @UpdateTimestamp
        var modified: Date = Date()
) {
    ...
}
```

- `Todo`:

```
package com.journaler.api.data

import com.fasterxml.jackson.annotation.JsonInclude
import org.hibernate.annotations.CreationTimestamp
import
 org.hibernate.annotations.GenericGenerator
import org.hibernate.annotations.UpdateTimestamp
```

```
import java.util.*
import javax.persistence.*

@Entity
@Table(name = "todo")
@JsonInclude(JsonInclude.Include.NON_NULL)
data class Todo(
        ...
        @CreationTimestamp
        var created: Date = Date(),
        @UpdateTimestamp
        var modified: Date = Date()
) {
    ...
}
```

With these timestamps, we will keep track of created/updated timestamps. Updating these two fields will be fully automatic. The user will not need to pass them every time the update operation it performed, but will be able to see it.

We also introduced the following annotation:

```
@JsonInclude(JsonInclude.Include.NON_NULL)
```

Thanks to this, we will ignore null fields during serialization. Create NoteDTO with the following implementation:

```
package com.journaler.api.data

import java.util.*

data class NoteDTO(
        var title: String,
        var message: String,
        var location: String = ""
) {

    var id: String = ""
    var created: Date = Date()
    var modified: Date = Date()

    constructor(note: Note) : this(
            note.title,
            note.message,
            note.location
    ) {
        id = note.id
```

```
        created = note.created
        modified = note.modified
    }
}
```

`TodoDTO` will be very similar, as follows:

```
package com.journaler.api.data

import java.util.*

data class TodoDTO(
        var title: String,
        var message: String,
        var schedule: Long,
        var location: String = ""
) {

    var id: String = ""
    var created: Date = Date()
    var modified: Date = Date()

    constructor(todo: Todo) : this(
            todo.title,
            todo.message,
            todo.schedule,
            todo.location
    ) {
        id = todo.id
        created = todo.created
        modified = todo.modified
    }
}
```

We have a main constructor containing mandatory and secondary fields that will convert the `Note` or `Todo` instance to its DTO equivalent.

We have to update our service and controller classes. Update your `NoteService` class to use DTO types:

```
@Service("Note service")
class NoteService {

    @Autowired
    lateinit var repository: NoteRepository

    fun getNotes(): Iterable<NoteDTO> = repository.findAll().map { it ->
```

```
NoteDTO(it) }

    fun insertNote(note: NoteDTO) = NoteDTO(
            repository.save(
                    Note(
                            title = note.title,
                            message = note.message,
                            location = note.location
                    )
            )
    )

    fun deleteNote(id: String) = repository.deleteById(id)

    fun updateNote(noteDto: NoteDTO): NoteDTO {
        var note = repository.findById(noteDto.id).get()
        note.title = noteDto.title
        note.message = noteDto.message
        note.location = noteDto.location
        note.modified = Date()
        note = repository.save(note)
        return NoteDTO(note)
    }
}
```

Do the same for the `TodoService` class:

```
@Service("Todo service")
class TodoService {

    @Autowired
    lateinit var repository: TodoRepository

    fun getTodos(): Iterable<TodoDTO> = repository.findAll().map { it ->
TodoDTO(it) }

    fun insertTodo(todo: TodoDTO): TodoDTO = TodoDTO(
            repository.save(
                    Todo(
                            title = todo.title,
                            message = todo.message,
                            location = todo.location,
                            schedule = todo.schedule

                    )
            )
    )
```

```
    fun deleteTodo(id: String) = repository.deleteById(id)

    fun updateTodo(todoDto: TodoDTO): TodoDTO {
        var todo = repository.findById(todoDto.id).get()
        todo.title = todoDto.title
        todo.message = todoDto.message
        todo.location = todoDto.location
        todo.schedule = todoDto.schedule
        todo.modified = Date()
        todo = repository.save(todo)
        return TodoDTO(todo)
    }
}
```

Finally, update your controllers. Update the NoteController class first:

```
@RestController
@RequestMapping("/notes")
class NoteController {

    @Autowired
    private lateinit var service: NoteService

    @GetMapping(
            produces = arrayOf(MediaType.APPLICATION_JSON_VALUE)
    )
    fun getNotes() = service.getNotes()

    @PutMapping(
            produces = arrayOf(MediaType.APPLICATION_JSON_VALUE),
            consumes = arrayOf(MediaType.APPLICATION_JSON_VALUE)
    )
    fun insertNote(
            @RequestBody note: NoteDTO
    ) = service.insertNote(note)

    @DeleteMapping(
            value = "/{id}",
            produces = arrayOf(MediaType.APPLICATION_JSON_VALUE)
    )
    fun deleteNote(
            @PathVariable(name = "id") id: String
    ) = service.deleteNote(id)

    @PostMapping(
            produces = arrayOf(MediaType.APPLICATION_JSON_VALUE),
            consumes = arrayOf(MediaType.APPLICATION_JSON_VALUE)
    )
```

```
    fun updateNote(
            @RequestBody note: NoteDTO
    ): NoteDTO = service.updateNote(note)
}
```

Change the `TodoController` class too:

```
 @RestController
@RequestMapping("/todos")
class TodoController {

    @Autowired
    private lateinit var service: TodoService

    @GetMapping(
            produces = arrayOf(MediaType.APPLICATION_JSON_VALUE)
    )
    fun getTodos(): Iterable<TodoDTO> = service.getTodos()

    @PutMapping(
            produces = arrayOf(MediaType.APPLICATION_JSON_VALUE),
            consumes = arrayOf(MediaType.APPLICATION_JSON_VALUE)
    )
    fun insertTodo(
            @RequestBody todo: TodoDTO
    ): TodoDTO = service.insertTodo(todo)

    @DeleteMapping(
            value = "/{id}",
            produces = arrayOf(MediaType.APPLICATION_JSON_VALUE)
    )
    fun deleteTodo(
            @PathVariable(name = "id") id: String
    ) = service.deleteTodo(id)

    @PostMapping(
            produces = arrayOf(MediaType.APPLICATION_JSON_VALUE),
            consumes = arrayOf(MediaType.APPLICATION_JSON_VALUE)
    )
    fun updateTodo(@RequestBody todo: TodoDTO): TodoDTO =
service.updateTodo(todo)

}
```

Build and run your application. Now try playing with the API calls. You can now create entities without passing all fields. Pay attention to the created/modified timestamps. They are automatically updated.

Creating database queries

Before we finish this chapter, we will introduce database queries to you. We will define several API calls that will trigger queries defined by us. Writing queries is simple. There are several ways to it. We will present the most common methodologies.

In the first example, we will introduce the API call that will query and return to us all the TODOs that are scheduled later than the date we provide. Open `TodoRepository` and extend it:

```
package com.journaler.api.repository

import com.journaler.api.data.Todo
import org.springframework.data.jpa.repository.Query
import org.springframework.data.repository.CrudRepository

/**
 * String is the type for ID we use.
 */
interface TodoRepository : CrudRepository<Todo, String> {

    @Query("from Todo t where t.schedule > ?1")
    fun findScheduledLaterThan(date: Long): Iterable<Todo>

}
```

We used `@Query` annotation to define our query with one parameter passed to it. As you can see, this query will return all TODOs that are scheduled later than the date provided. Now open `TodoService` and introduce a new method:

```
fun getScheduledLaterThan(date: Date): Iterable<TodoDTO> {
        return repository.findScheduledLaterThan(date.time).map { it ->
TodoDTO(it) }
}
```

Finally, let's connect this with the `TodoController` class:

```
package com.journaler.api.controller

import com.journaler.api.data.TodoDTO
import com.journaler.api.service.TodoService
import org.springframework.beans.factory.annotation.Autowired
import org.springframework.http.MediaType
import org.springframework.web.bind.annotation.*

@RestController
@RequestMapping("/todos")
class TodoController {
    ...
    fun getTodosLaterThan(
            @RequestBody payload: TodoLaterThanRequest
    ): Iterable<TodoDTO> = service.getScheduledLaterThan(payload.date)
}
```

We introduced a new class here. We introduced a data class so we can pass the date to API calls. Create a `TodoLaterThanRequest` class and locate it under the controller package. The class should have a simple definition:

```
package com.journaler.api.controller
import java.util.*
data class TodoLaterThanRequest(val date: Date)
```

Build and run your application. Make sure you have inserted several TODOs with proper dates set for the schedule field. If you try an API call, you will get all the items that satisfy the conditions we defined in our query:

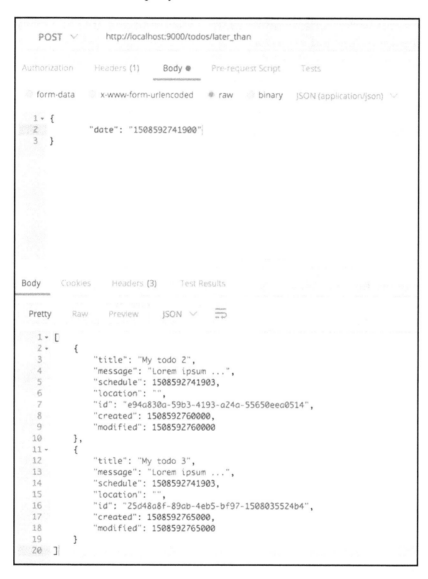

Named queries

We will give one more example of querying data. We will introduce you to named queries. We will define named queries by using the `@NamedQuery` annotation applied to our entity class. To give you a better understanding of what we are talking about, we will extend our code. Open the `Note` class and extend it:

```
package com.journaler.api.data
...
@Entity
@Table(name = "note")
@JsonInclude(JsonInclude.Include.NON_NULL)
@NamedQuery(
        name = "Note.findByTitle",
        query = "SELECT n FROM Note n WHERE n.title LIKE ?1"
)
data class Note(
    ...
) {
    ...
}
```

We defined a query that will find all Notes with the title we provide as a parameter through API call. The method that will trigger a query is called `findByTitle`, so it must be defined in our `NoteRepository`:

```
...
interface NoteRepository : CrudRepository<Note, String> {
    fun findByTitle(title: String): Iterable<Note>
}
```

What is left is to connect it with `NoteService` by adding the method:

```
fun findByTitle(title: String): Iterable<NoteDTO> {
        return repository.findByTitle(title).map { it -> NoteDTO(it) }
}
```

And connecting the service to the controller class:

```
...
@RestController
@RequestMapping("/notes")
class NoteController {
    ...
    @PostMapping(
            value = "/by_title",
            produces = arrayOf(MediaType.APPLICATION_JSON_VALUE),
```

```
        consumes = arrayOf(MediaType.APPLICATION_JSON_VALUE)

    )
    fun getTodosLaterThan(
            @RequestBody payload: NoteFindByTitleRequest
    ): Iterable<NoteDTO> = service.findByTitle(payload.title)

}
```

As you can see, we also defined the `NoteFindByTitleRequest` class for the payload:

```
package com.journaler.api.controller

data class NoteFindByTitleRequest(val title: String)
```

Build and run your application. If you try a newly created API call, you should be able to search Notes by a `title`, just as we did:

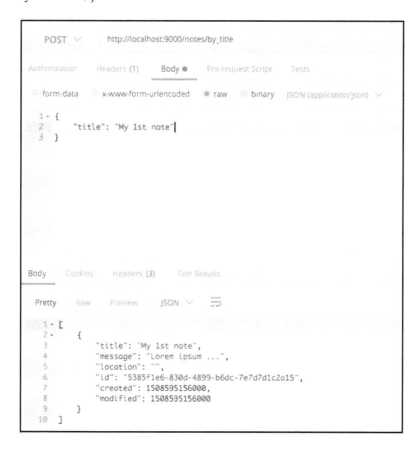

Summary

In this chapter, we introduced you to Spring Data JPA and MySQL. We created all classes needed to establish communication with the database. We didn't just make CRUD operations possible, but also demonstrated how to write custom queries for our application. In the next chapter, we will move one step forward in Spring development. We will limit access to certain parts of our API by introducing Spring Security.

5
Securing Applications with Spring Security

In this chapter, we will cover the basics of Spring Security. This is a huge part of Spring Framework so take your time. We will cover the following topics:

- Introducing Spring Security
- Defining user roles
- Defining **data transfer objects** (**DTOs**) for users
- Providing authentication
- Providing authorization

Introducing Spring Security

As the name suggests, Spring Security represents the framework with various security-related power features. It offers a highly customizable authentication and access control framework. In modern development, Spring Security is a de facto standard for securing Spring Framework-based applications.

Spring Security provides not just authentication but authorization features to the application. Spring Security comes with the following features:

- Authentication and authorization
- Basic, digest, and form-based authentication
- LDAP authentication
- OpenID authentication
- Single Sign-On implementation

- **Cross-Site Request Forgery** (**CSRF**) implementation
- Remember-Me through HTTP cookies
- ACLs implementation
- Channel Security, automatically switching between HTTP and HTTPS
- I18N internationalization
- JAAS, Java Authentication, and Authorization Service
- Flow Authorization using Spring WebFlow Framework
- WS-Security using Spring Web Services
- Configuration through both XML and Annotations
- WebSocket Security
- Spring Data Integration
- CSRF Token Argument Resolver

As you can see, there is plenty that Spring Security has to offer in the security area. Our primary focus will be on Basic Authentication and OAuth2, to be able to utilize its proper dependencies. Open your `build.grade` configuration and extend it:

```
...
dependencies {
    compile 'org.springframework.boot:spring-boot-starter-security'
    ...
}
```

Defining user roles

Next, we are going to define some user roles. We will define the user role and what API calls that role can execute. So, we will have the following roles:

- `ADMIN`: Can execute all the API calls and also create, update or remove users
- `MEMBER`: Represents a regular system user and can execute all API calls except user-related ones

A user with no role (not logged in) can't execute any API calls.

Defining classes for each role

We have scoped our roles, so we need to create proper classes. Create a new package called security. The first class we will create will be the class that represents user definition. Create a class called User and make sure it extends the UserDetails class from the org.springframework.security.core.userdetails package:

```
package com.journaler.api.security

...
import org.springframework.security.core.GrantedAuthority
import org.springframework.security.core.userdetails.UserDetails
...

open class User : UserDetails {

    override fun getAuthorities(): MutableCollection<out GrantedAuthority>
{
        ...
    }

    override fun isEnabled(): Boolean {
        ...
    }

    override fun getUsername(): String {
        ...
    }

    override fun isCredentialsNonExpired(): Boolean {
        ...
    }

    override fun getPassword(): String {
        ...
    }

    override fun isAccountNonExpired(): Boolean {
        ...
    }

    override fun isAccountNonLocked(): Boolean {
        ...
    }
}
```

Extending the `UserDetails` class provides the core user's information. Implementation is not used directly by Spring Security for security purposes. It's simply used to store the user's information, which is later encapsulated into authentication implementation objects (imported from `org.springframework.security.core.Authentication`).

This makes it possible for nonsecurity-related user information (such as email addresses, and telephone numbers) to be stored.

As you can see, the `UserDetails` class forces us to override the following methods:

- `getAuthorities()` returns the authorities granted to the user. It cannot return null!
- `isEnabled()` indicates whether the user is enabled or disabled. A disabled user cannot be authenticated.
- `getUsername()` returns the username used to authenticate the user. It cannot return null!
- `isCredentialsNonExpired()` indicates whether the user's credentials (password) have expired or not. Expired credentials prevent authentication.
- `getPassword()` returns the password used to authenticate the user.
- `isAccountNonExpired()` indicates whether the user's account has expired. An expired account cannot be authenticated.
- `isAccountNonLocked()` indicates whether the user is locked or unlocked. A locked user cannot be authenticated.

We will implement our `User` class like this:

```
package com.journaler.api.security

import com.fasterxml.jackson.annotation.JsonInclude
import com.fasterxml.jackson.annotation.JsonProperty
import org.hibernate.annotations.CreationTimestamp
import org.hibernate.annotations.GenericGenerator
import org.hibernate.annotations.UpdateTimestamp
import org.hibernate.validator.constraints.Email
import org.hibernate.validator.constraints.NotBlank
import org.springframework.security.core.GrantedAuthority
import org.springframework.security.core.authority.SimpleGrantedAuthority
import org.springframework.security.core.userdetails.UserDetails
import java.util.*
import javax.persistence.*
import javax.validation.constraints.NotNull

@Entity
```

```kotlin
@Table(name = "user")
@JsonInclude(JsonInclude.Include.NON_NULL)
open class User(
        @Id
        @GeneratedValue(generator = "uuid2")
        @GenericGenerator(name = "uuid2", strategy = "uuid2")
        @Column(columnDefinition = "varchar(36)")
        var id: String = "",

        @Column(unique = true, nullable = false)
        @NotNull
        @Email
        var email: String = "",

        @JsonProperty(access = JsonProperty.Access.WRITE_ONLY)
        @NotBlank
        var pwd: String = "",

        @NotBlank
        var firstName: String = "",

        @NotBlank
        var lastName: String = "",

        var roles: String = "",
        var enabled: Boolean = true,
        var accountNonExpired: Boolean = true,
        var accountNonLocked: Boolean = true,
        var credentialsNonExpired: Boolean = true,

        @CreationTimestamp
        var created: Date = Date(),

        @UpdateTimestamp
        var modified: Date = Date()
) : UserDetails {

    /**
     * We need empty constructor for SecurityInitializationTest and
Hibernate.
     */
    constructor() : this(
            "", "", "", "", "", "", true, true, true, true, Date(), Date()
    )

    override fun getAuthorities(): MutableCollection<out GrantedAuthority>
{
        val authorities = mutableListOf<GrantedAuthority>()
```

```
        roles
                .split(",")
                .forEach { it ->
                    authorities.add(
                            SimpleGrantedAuthority(
                                    it.trim()
                            )
                    )
                }
        return authorities
    }

    override fun isEnabled() = enabled

    override fun getUsername() = email

    override fun isCredentialsNonExpired() = credentialsNonExpired

    override fun getPassword() = pwd

    override fun isAccountNonExpired() = accountNonExpired

    override fun isAccountNonLocked() = accountNonLocked

}
```

There are a few important notes. We consider the User class to be an entity, so it will be stored in the database. The @Email annotation tells the framework to check that the email for validation. The @NotBlank annotation will prevent us from sending invalid data. @NotBlank checks the value is not null or empty. Spring trims the value first. Like this, it's not possible to pass empty spaces. We will use this opportunity to mention two more important annotations:

- @NotNull, to verify that the value is not null, disregarding the content.
- @NotEmpty, to verify that the value is not null or empty. If it has just empty spaces, it will allow it as not empty!

Build and run your Spring application and then check the tables and the structure of the database. You will notice one more table named user with the following structure:

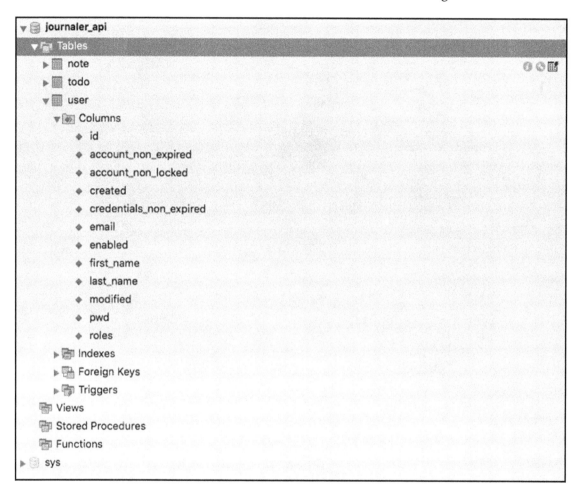

To cover the ADMIN role, we must introduce one more class. Create a class named Admin in the same package in which you created the User class:

```
package com.journaler.api.security

import java.util.*
import javax.persistence.DiscriminatorValue
import javax.persistence.Entity

@Entity
```

```
@DiscriminatorValue(value = "ADMIN")
class Admin(
        id: String,
        email: String,
        pwd: String,
        firstName: String,
        lastName: String,
        roles: String,
        enabled: Boolean,
        accountNonExpired: Boolean,
        accountNonLocked: Boolean,
        credentialsNonExpired: Boolean,
        created: Date,
        modified: Date
) : User(
        id,
        email,
        pwd,
        firstName,
        lastName,
        roles,
        enabled,
        accountNonExpired,
        accountNonLocked,
        credentialsNonExpired,
        created,
        modified
) {

    /**
     * We need empty constructor for SecurityInitializationTest and
Hibernate.
     */
    constructor() : this(
            "", "", "", "", "", "", true, true, true, true, Date(), Date()
    )

}
```

Run your application one more time and take a look at the changes that occurred in the
user table:

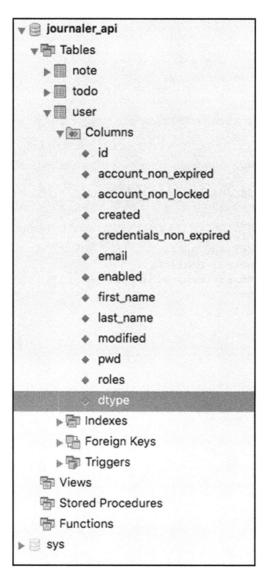

As you can see, there is now one more field: dtype.

We must implement a `Member` class, too, so we cover our MEMBER role. Create a `Member` class and make sure it's implemented like this:

```
package com.journaler.api.security

import java.util.*
import javax.persistence.DiscriminatorValue
import javax.persistence.Entity

@Entity
@DiscriminatorValue(value = "MEMBER")
class Member(
        id: String,
        email: String,
        pwd: String,
        firstName: String,
        lastName: String,
        roles: String,
        enabled: Boolean,
        accountNonExpired: Boolean,
        accountNonLocked: Boolean,
        credentialsNonExpired: Boolean,
        created: Date,
        modified: Date
) : User(
        id,
        email,
        pwd,
        firstName,
        lastName,
        roles,
        enabled,
        accountNonExpired,
        accountNonLocked,
        credentialsNonExpired,
        created,
        modified
) {

    /**
     * We need empty constructor for SecurityInitializationTest and
Hibernate.
     */
```

```
constructor() : this(
        "", "", "", "", "", "", true, true, true, true, Date(), Date()
)
```

```
}
```

The `Member` class has the same implementation as the `Admin` class but it will be used in the context of different roles.

Defining DTOs for the user

We will need DTOs to achieve maximal flexibility for all user-related operations that we will define. The first DTO will be the one we use when it returns a list of available users in the system. Define a new class called `UserDetailsDTO`:

```
package com.journaler.api.security

import java.util.*

data class UserDetailsDTO(
        val id: String,
        var email: String,
        var firstName: String,
        var lastName: String,
        var roles: String,
        var enabled: Boolean,
        var accountNonExpired: Boolean,
        var accountNonLocked: Boolean,
        var credentialsNonExpired: Boolean,
        var created: Date,
        var modified: Date
)
```

`UserDetailsDTO` is a simple data class containing only mandatory fields. As you can see, we will not return back the password value. For saving a new user, we will define another data class called `UserDTO`:

```
package com.journaler.api.security

data class UserDTO(
        var email: String,
        var password: String,
        var firstName: String,
        var lastName: String
)
```

We will use it when creating a new user in the system. Only these four fields will be provided. The other fields will be auto-populated, or will use default values.

To be able to save users in the database, we need a repository. Create `UserRepository`:

```
package com.journaler.api.repository

import com.journaler.api.security.User
import org.springframework.data.repository.CrudRepository

interface UserRepository : CrudRepository<User, String> {

    fun findOneByEmail(email: String): User?

}
```

To be able to locate the user by their username (email address in our case), we must have a `findOneByEmail()` method.

To be able to get a list of users or to create new ones, we need to define the API calls for user-related needs. We will have the following calls:

- [GET], /users returns a list of users in the system
- [PUT], /users/admin inserts a new admin user
- [PUT], /users/member inserts a new member user
- [DELETE], /users/{id} removes a user with ID from the system
- [POST], /users updates users in the system

All user-related operations will be performed in the `UserService` class:

```
package com.journaler.api.service

import com.journaler.api.repository.UserRepository
import com.journaler.api.security.*
import org.springframework.beans.factory.annotation.Autowired
import org.springframework.security.core.userdetails.UserDetailsService
import org.springframework.security.crypto.bcrypt.BCryptPasswordEncoder
import org.springframework.stereotype.Repository
import java.util.*

@Repository
class UserService : UserDetailsService {

    @Autowired
    lateinit var repository: UserRepository
```

```
    val encoder = BCryptPasswordEncoder(11)

    override fun loadUserByUsername(email: String): User? {
        return repository.findOneByEmail(email) ?: throw
RuntimeException("User not found: $email")
    }

    fun saveMember(user: UserDTO): User {
        val member = Member()
        member.email = user.email
        member.firstName = user.firstName
        member.lastName = user.lastName
        member.pwd = encoder.encode(user.password)
        member.roles = "MEMBER"
        return repository.save(member)
    }

    fun saveAdmin(user: UserDTO): User {
        val admin = Admin()
        admin.email = user.email
        admin.firstName = user.firstName
        admin.lastName = user.lastName
        admin.roles = "ADMIN, MEMBER"
        admin.pwd = encoder.encode(user.password)
        return repository.save(admin)
    }

    fun updateUser(toSave: User): User? {
        val user = repository.findOneByEmail(toSave.email)
        user?.let {
            if (!toSave.pwd.isEmpty()) {
                user.pwd = encoder.encode(toSave.password)
            }
            user.firstName = toSave.firstName
            user.lastName = toSave.lastName
            user.accountNonExpired = toSave.accountNonExpired
            user.accountNonLocked = toSave.accountNonLocked
            user.credentialsNonExpired = toSave.credentialsNonExpired
            user.modified = Date()
            return repository.save(user)
        }
        return null
    }

    fun getUsers() = repository.findAll().map { it ->
        UserDetailsDTO(
                it.id,
                it.email,
```

```
                    it.firstName,
                    it.lastName,
                    it.roles,
                    it.enabled,
                    it.accountNonExpired,
                    it.accountNonLocked,
                    it.credentialsNonExpired,
                    it.created,
                    it.modified
            )
    }

    fun deleteUser(id: String) = repository.deleteById(id)

}
```

The `userService` will perform all CRUD operations. In order to trigger any of them, we need to finally connect `UserService` with `UserController`, which will define all API calls we planned:

```
package com.journaler.api.controller

import com.journaler.api.security.User
import com.journaler.api.security.UserDTO
import com.journaler.api.service.UserService
import org.springframework.beans.factory.annotation.Autowired
import org.springframework.http.MediaType
import org.springframework.web.bind.annotation.*

@RestController
@RequestMapping("/users")
class UserController {

    @Autowired
    lateinit var service: UserService

    @GetMapping(
            produces = arrayOf(MediaType.APPLICATION_JSON_VALUE)
    )
    fun getUsers() = service.getUsers()

    @PutMapping(
            value = "/admin",
            produces = arrayOf(MediaType.APPLICATION_JSON_VALUE),
            consumes = arrayOf(MediaType.APPLICATION_JSON_VALUE)
    )
    fun insertAdmin(
```

```kotlin
        @RequestBody user: UserDTO
) = service.saveAdmin(user)

@PutMapping(
        value = "/member",
        produces = arrayOf(MediaType.APPLICATION_JSON_VALUE),
        consumes = arrayOf(MediaType.APPLICATION_JSON_VALUE)
)
fun insertMember(
        @RequestBody user: UserDTO
) = service.saveMember(user)


@DeleteMapping(
        value = "/{id}",
        produces = arrayOf(MediaType.APPLICATION_JSON_VALUE)
)
fun deleteUser(
        @PathVariable(name = "id") id: String
) = service.deleteUser(id)

@PostMapping(
        produces = arrayOf(MediaType.APPLICATION_JSON_VALUE),
        consumes = arrayOf(MediaType.APPLICATION_JSON_VALUE)
)
fun updateUser(
        @RequestBody user: User
): User? = service.updateUser(user)

}
```

By now, we have all the user-related stuff ready but nothing is yet secured. If you run your application, you will be able to execute any API call without any authentication.

Securing your REST API with basic authentication

To be able to authenticate and authorize users, we will add basic authentication implementation. By default, Spring will handle /login as a web page and that is something we don't want for our REST API. Create a new class inside the security package and call it WebSecurityEntryPoint.

This class must implement the `AuthenticationEntryPoint` interface whose purpose is to commence an authentication scheme. The implementation will look like this:

```
package com.journaler.api.security

import org.springframework.security.core.AuthenticationException
import org.springframework.security.web.AuthenticationEntryPoint
import org.springframework.stereotype.Component
import javax.servlet.http.HttpServletRequest
import javax.servlet.http.HttpServletResponse

@Component
class WebSecurityEntryPoint : AuthenticationEntryPoint {

    override fun commence(
            request: HttpServletRequest?,
            response: HttpServletResponse?,
            authException: AuthenticationException?
    ) {
        response?.sendError(HttpServletResponse.SC_UNAUTHORIZED, "Access
Denied")
    }

}
```

So, what does the `commence()` method do? As its name suggests, it commences an authentication scheme. Spring Security handles authentication by automatically triggering the authentication process with the concept of **Entry Point**. Entry Point is a required part of the configuration and can be injected. Our Entry Point implementation will simply return 401 whenever it's triggered.

We also need an authentication success handler. The class will be responsible for handling authentication results. Create a new class called `WebSecurityAuthSuccessHandler` and make sure it extends the `SimpleUrlAuthenticationSuccessHandler` class:

```
package com.journaler.api.security

import org.springframework.security.core.Authentication
import
org.springframework.security.web.authentication.SimpleUrlAuthenticationSucc
essHandler
import
org.springframework.security.web.savedrequest.HttpSessionRequestCache
import org.springframework.stereotype.Component
import org.springframework.util.StringUtils
import javax.servlet.http.HttpServletRequest
```

```
import javax.servlet.http.HttpServletResponse

@Component
class WebSecurityAuthSuccessHandler :
SimpleUrlAuthenticationSuccessHandler() {

    var requestCache = HttpSessionRequestCache()

    override fun onAuthenticationSuccess(
            request: HttpServletRequest,
            response: HttpServletResponse,
            authentication: Authentication
    ) {
        val savedRequest = requestCache.getRequest(request, response)
        if (savedRequest == null) {
            clearAuthenticationAttributes(request)
            return
        }
        val parameter = request.getParameter(targetUrlParameter)
        val ok = isAlwaysUseDefaultTargetUrl ||
                    targetUrlParameter != null &&
                    StringUtils.hasText(parameter)
        if (ok) {
            requestCache.removeRequest(request, response)
            clearAuthenticationAttributes(request)
            return
        }
        clearAuthenticationAttributes(request)
    }

}
```

We define the fact that the desired response for a successful authentication should be 200 OK. We will inject authentication success handler implementation to replace the default. The default would perform a redirect, but since we are making a REST API, we don't need that, only the success response.

Let's tie things together and configure Spring Security! To configure Spring Security, we need to create a Spring configuration class that extends `WebSecurityConfigurerAdapter`. Create a new class called `WebSecurityConfiguration`:

```
package com.journaler.api.security

import com.journaler.api.service.UserService
import org.springframework.beans.factory.annotation.Autowired
import org.springframework.context.annotation.Bean
```

```
import org.springframework.context.annotation.Configuration
import org.springframework.security.access.AccessDecisionManager
import org.springframework.security.access.vote.AuthenticatedVoter
import org.springframework.security.access.vote.RoleVoter
import org.springframework.security.access.vote.UnanimousBased
import
org.springframework.security.config.annotation.web.configuration.EnableWebS
ecurity
import
org.springframework.security.config.annotation.web.configuration.WebSecurit
yConfigurerAdapter
import
org.springframework.security.config.annotation.authentication.builders.Auth
enticationManagerBuilder
import org.springframework.security.crypto.bcrypt.BCryptPasswordEncoder
import org.springframework.security.crypto.password.PasswordEncoder
import
org.springframework.security.authentication.dao.DaoAuthenticationProvider
import
org.springframework.security.config.annotation.web.builders.HttpSecurity
import org.springframework.security.web.AuthenticationEntryPoint
import
org.springframework.security.web.access.expression.WebExpressionVoter
import
org.springframework.security.web.authentication.SimpleUrlAuthenticationFail
ureHandler
import java.util.*


@Configuration
@EnableWebSecurity
class WebSecurityConfiguration : WebSecurityConfigurerAdapter() {

    @Autowired
    lateinit var service: UserService

    /**
     * Will be resolved into: WebSecurityEntryPoint injected instance.
     */
    @Autowired
    lateinit var unauthorizedHandler: AuthenticationEntryPoint

    @Autowired
    lateinit var successHandler: WebSecurityAuthSuccessHandler

    @Autowired
    override fun configure(auth: AuthenticationManagerBuilder) {
        auth.authenticationProvider(authenticationProvider())
```

```
    }

    override fun configure(http: HttpSecurity?) {
        http
                ?.csrf()?.disable()
                ?.exceptionHandling()
                ?.authenticationEntryPoint(unauthorizedHandler)
                ?.and()
                ?.authorizeRequests()
                /**
                 * Access to Notes and Todos API calls is given to any
authenticated system user.
                 */
                ?.antMatchers("/notes")?.authenticated()
                ?.antMatchers("/notes/**")?.authenticated()
                ?.antMatchers("/todos")?.authenticated()
                ?.antMatchers("/todos/**")?.authenticated()
                /**
                 * Access to User API calls is given only to Admin user.
                 */
                ?.antMatchers("/users")?.hasAnyAuthority("ADMIN")
                ?.antMatchers("/users/**")?.hasAnyAuthority("ADMIN")
                ?.and()
                ?.formLogin()
                ?.successHandler(successHandler)
                ?.failureHandler(SimpleUrlAuthenticationFailureHandler())
                ?.and()
                ?.logout()
    }

    @Bean
    fun authenticationProvider(): DaoAuthenticationProvider {
        val authProvider = DaoAuthenticationProvider()
        authProvider.setUserDetailsService(service)
        authProvider.setPasswordEncoder(encoder())
        return authProvider
    }

    @Bean
    fun encoder(): PasswordEncoder = BCryptPasswordEncoder(11)

    @Bean
    fun accessDecisionManager(): AccessDecisionManager {
        val decisionVoters = Arrays.asList(
                WebExpressionVoter(),
                RoleVoter(),
                AuthenticatedVoter()
        )
```

```
        return UnanimousBased(decisionVoters)
    }
}
```

Let's explain what we just did. If you look from the bottom of the class implementation, you will notice the following methods:

- The `authenticationProvider()` method will provide us with the instance of the `DaoAuthenticationProvider` class that will be used for authentication purposes. We assigned `UserService` as the mechanism to retrieve users. We also assigned a password encoder obtained by triggering the `encoder()` method.
- The `encoder()` method will provide us with the instance of the `BCryptPasswordEncoder` class used to perform password encryption. The BCrypt strong hashing function will be used for encryption.
- The `accessDecisionManager()` method will provide an `AccessDecisionManager` instance. The `AccessDecisionManager` abstract class is responsible for authorization. We will return a new instance of the `UnanimousBased` class that requires all voters to abstain or grants access. The constructor accepts a list of `AccessDecisionVoter` instances. Each `AccessDecisionVoter` represents the implementation responsible for voting on authorization decisions. We will use the following implementations:
  - `WebExpressionVoter`: `AccessDecisionVoter` implementation that handles web authorization decisions.
  - `RoleVoter`: `AccessDecisionVoter` implementation that votes if any configuration attribute starts with a prefix indicating that it is a role.
  - `AuthenticatedVoter`: `AccessDecisionVoter` implementation that votes if any configuration attribute is present: `IS_AUTHENTICATED_FULLY`, `IS_AUTHENTICATED_REMEMBERED`, `IS_AUTHENTICATED_ANONYMOUSLY`.

By using this combination of voters, we will be able to authenticate and authorize users. Before you try the code we implemented, you need the database to be populated with some users. We need at least one user with an ADMIN role and at least one user with a MEMBER role. For that purpose, we will create a test that will instantiate and insert users into the database. We will not go into the details of this test since we will cover testing in Chapter 9, *Testing*.

Locate the test directory of your project (/src/test) and create a test class under the test package (src/test/kotlin/com/journaler/api) named SecurityInitializationTest with the following implementation:

```kotlin
package com.journaler.api

import com.journaler.api.security.Admin
import com.journaler.api.security.Member
import com.journaler.api.security.UserDTO
import com.journaler.api.service.UserService
import org.junit.Assert
import org.junit.Test
import org.junit.runner.RunWith
import org.springframework.beans.factory.annotation.Autowired
import org.springframework.boot.test.context.SpringBootTest
import org.springframework.test.context.junit4.SpringRunner

@RunWith(SpringRunner::class)
@SpringBootTest
class SecurityInitializationTest {

    @Autowired
    private lateinit var userService: UserService
    private val password = "12345"
    private val adminEmail = "admin@example.com"
    private val memberEmail = "member@example.com"

    @Test
    fun initAdmin() {
        try {
            val admin = userService.loadUserByUsername(adminEmail)
            if (admin is Admin) {
                println("Admin user exists: ${admin.id}")
            } else {
                Assert.fail("Admin is not an admin.")
            }
```

```
        } catch (e: RuntimeException) {
            val toSave = UserDTO(
                    adminEmail,
                    password,
                    "admin",
                    "admin"
            )
            val saved = userService.saveAdmin(toSave)
            println("Admin user inserted: ${saved.id}")
        }
    }

    @Test
    fun initMember() {
        try {
            val member = userService.loadUserByUsername(memberEmail)
            if (member is Member) {
                println("Member user exists: ${member.id}")
            } else {
                Assert.fail("Member is not an member.")
            }
        } catch (e: RuntimeException) {
            val toSave = UserDTO(
                    memberEmail,
                    password,
                    "member",
                    "member"
            )
            val saved = userService.saveMember(toSave)
            println("Member user inserted: ${saved.id}")
        }
    }
}
```

Run your test (right-click on the `SecurityInitializationTest.kt` and click on the **Run 'SecurityInitializationTest'** option). It will take some time to initialize Spring Boot and execute the test, as shown in the following screenshot:

When done, check the content of your database:

As you can see, there are two users inserted. Use `username` and `password` from the test code to authenticate. Let's try to log in. Open Postman and authenticate:

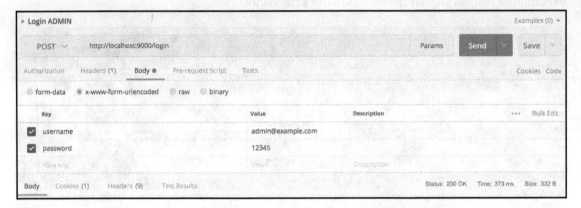

Take your time and play with API calls with Spring Security introduced to our project.

What else can Spring Security do?

Spring Security is huge! With Spring Security, it is possible to achieve much more than we just presented. Let's highlight some great Spring Security features.

For example, you can define your own authorization provider and authorization rules or, for example, support LDAP or OpenID authentication easily with very few lines of code.

With Spring Security, you can encode and validate passwords. Classes must implement the `PasswordEncoder` interface:

```
package org.springframework.security.crypto.password;

/**
 * Service interface for encoding passwords.
 *
 * The preferred implementation is {@code BCryptPasswordEncoder}.
 *
 * @author Keith Donald
 */
public interface PasswordEncoder {

    /**
     * Encode the raw password. Generally, a good encoding algorithm applies
     a SHA-1 or
```

```
   * greater hash combined with an 8-byte or greater randomly generated
salt.
   */
  String encode(CharSequence rawPassword);

  /**
   * Verify the encoded password obtained from storage matches the
submitted raw
   * password after it too is encoded. Returns true if the passwords
match, false if
   * they do not. The stored password itself is never decoded.
   *
   * @param rawPassword the raw password to encode and match
   * @param encodedPassword the encoded password from storage to compare
with
   * @return true if the raw password, after encoding, matches the encoded
password from
   * storage
   */
  boolean matches(CharSequence rawPassword, String encodedPassword);

}
```

These are the most commonly used implementations:

- BaseDigestPasswordEncoder
- BasePasswordEncoder
- BCryptPasswordEncoder
- LdapShaPasswordEncoder
- Md4PasswordEncoder
- Md5PasswordEncoder
- MessageDigestPasswordEncoder
- MessageDigestPasswordEncoder
- PlaintextPasswordEncoder
- ShaPasswordEncoder

As you have probably noticed, in our example we used BCryptPasswordEncoder implementation.

It is important to note that it is possible to perform method-level security using annotations, for example:

- `@RolesAllowed({"ROLE_MEMBER","ROLE_ADMIN"})`
- `@PermitAll`
- `@DenyAll`

With the examples we have covered in this chapter, we have just touched on the basics of Spring Security. Do not be scared since it will take you time to master it. Spring Security requires some time to learn and to discover all its possibilities. Be patient and try to write as much code as you can! Read Spring Security-related literature and do not rush. You will be a Spring Security master!

Summary

Secure applications are a must! Spring provides us with the perfect tools for that purpose. Spring Security, as a highly customizable authentication and access control framework, was an excellent choice to achieve this. We demonstrated how to do basic to advanced security setup and how to prevent unauthorized use of our API calls. In the next chapter, we will show you Spring Cloud and how to achieve some common needs in distributed systems.

6
Spring Cloud

Hi there! Can you believe that we are already halfway through this book? The next topic we are going to introduce you to is Spring Cloud. Spring Cloud is one of the most important features Spring has to offer. Why do we need it? Spring Cloud provides us with tools to build some of the most necessary patterns in distributed systems. By using Spring Cloud, we will avoid boilerplate code when coordinating our distributed systems. In this chapter, we will guide you in achieving some of the most commonly used configurations.

In this chapter, you will learn about the following:

- Microservice architecture
- Microservice with Spring Cloud
- Spring Cloud in practice
- Updating API application
- Securing Spring Cloud services

Microservice architecture versus SOA

SOA stands for service-oriented architecture. To remind you, in short, SOA can be defined by the following points:

- Services are autonomous
- Their boundaries are explicit
- Services share schemas and contracts (not class)
- Service compatibility is based on the policy

In SOA, several different services (smaller applications) can be combined to act as one single big application. This gives us the conclusion that by using SOA, we achieve modularity for our software. Services in SOA pass and parse messages by protocols that describe them.

Based on this, we can explain microservices with respect to SOA. Microservices represent the interpretation of SOA, which is used to build distributed systems. Services in a microservice architecture are processes that communicate with each other. You must have noted that there is no single commonly agreed definition of microservices. Therefore, we will highlight the following characteristics and principles that are most commonly mentioned:

- Delicate interfaces for deploying services independently
- Business-driven development, for example, domain-driven design
- Polyglot programming
- Persistence
- Lightweight container deployment
- IDEAL cloud application architectures
- Decentralized continuous delivery
- Holistic service monitoring for DevOps

Understanding microservice architectures

Let's put more focus on microservice architecture. It's the most commonly used architecture in modern enterprise application development. Since it is scalable, it is considered one of the best approaches for the development of this kind.

The first key point in understanding microservices is that the whole system must be broken into multiple independent applications. What are the benefits of this? Each application (service) can be easily and independently deployed, maintained, and redeployed as needed.

Each microservice has a single responsibility, which is its primary context. For example, development teams can be focused independently on the development of certain contexts and sets of features. Microservices receive requests, process them, and send responses to the pipes though which information flows.

One of the important points to understand is that microservices can experience certain failures. Since they depend on each other and the processed data, handling these failures can increase their complexity.

So, let's summarize this! The microservice architecture uses services as components. Each of the services is organized around a certain business context. They have smart endpoints but very simple information flow mechanisms. Governance is decentralized as well as data management.

Microservices with Spring Cloud

We will consider our API as a piece of a puzzle. Let's say it will be one of the services in the microservice architecture. What we want to achieve is to make it possible to easily work in any distributed environment. Spring Cloud builds on Spring Boot and provides sets of libraries that extend the abilities of our application when added to the classpath.

Spring Cloud provides the following features:

- **Distributed and versioned configuration**: Spring Cloud configuration provides server and client-side support for configuration externalization. We define the configuration server as the central place to manage external properties for applications across all environments.
- **Service registration and discovery**: We need a way for all of our servers to be able to find each other. Spring Cloud makes this possible and easy to do.
- **Routing and filtering**: With routing and filtering, the Spring Cloud feature microservice application can work as a reverse proxy. Microservices can forward requests to the other service application. With the same microservice, it's also possible to apply proper filtering so that maximal flexibility is achieved.
- **Calls service-to-service**: Spring Cloud makes it possible to easily establish communication between microservices. For this purpose, Spring Cloud offers direct support for Eureka! Besides this support, Spring Cloud supports the following integrations, too:
  - Hystrix
  - Zuul
  - Archaius and many others
- **Load balancing**: Every modern system requires load balancing—especially systems with big traffic. Thanks to Spring Cloud, we can implement a microservice application that uses Netflix Ribbon and Spring Cloud Netflix to provide client-side load balancing in calls to another microservice.
- **Circuit breakers**: Spring Cloud supports circuit breaker pattern implementation. So, with the use of the circuit breaker pattern, we can allow a microservice to continue operating even when a related service is failing! By doing this, we prevent the failure from cascading.
- **Leadership election and cluster state**: Leadership election allows microservices to work together with other microservices so that they can coordinate a cluster leadership via a third-party system. A leader can then be used to provide a global state or global ordering with high availability.

- **Distributed messaging**: Spring Cloud Bus connects our microservices with a lightweight message broker. Thanks to this, we can broadcast state changes or other instructions. With this, huge flexibility is achieved without the need for boilerplate code.

Each of these features represents the requirements that any serious enterprise system needs. Before we dive into the most important ones, we will give a brief explanation so that you are aware of what you can create.

Spring Cloud in practice

Finally, it's time to show you how to use Spring Cloud. We are going to extend our project and introduce the implementations for the most frequently used Spring Cloud components. To be able to use it, extend the `build.gradle` configuration with the Spring Cloud dependency:

```
buildscript {
    ext {
        kotlinVersion = '1.1.60'
        springBootVersion = '2.0.0.M6'
    }
    ...
}

...

repositories {
    ...
}

dependencies {
    ...
    // compile 'org.springframework.cloud:spring-cloud-config-server'
    ...
}

dependencyManagement {
    imports {
        mavenBom "org.springframework.cloud:spring-cloud-
dependencies:Finchley.M4"
    }
}
```

As you can see, we upgraded Spring Boot version 2.0.0.M4 to 2.0.0.M6. We also added (for now, under the comments) the `spring-cloud-config-server` dependency and a `dependencyManagement` import for `spring-cloud-dependencies:Finchley.M4`.

Build and run your project to make sure nothing is broken. We are now ready to develop some serious Spring Cloud stuff!

The first Spring Cloud feature we want to support will be distributed configuration. For this purpose, we must define the following:

- **Configuration server**: Here, we will define our configuration application responsible for providing configurations to all other applications (microservices), and then we will connect to it to obtain proper application configuration. We will present to you a simple implementation so that you can understand this concept.
- **Discovery**: Here, we need a mechanism so that all of our servers are be able to find each other. We will resolve this by running the Eureka discovery server.
- **Gateway**: To resolve the problem of clients accessing all of our defined applications, we will create a gateway. The gateway will behave as a reverse proxy, managing requests from clients to our servers.

Configuration server

Let's create a Spring project for configuration server. We will define a blank application with Spring Cloud dependencies. Later, we will add code, representing server configuration implementation. The application will belong to the following context:

```
com.journaler.config
```

Make sure your application is defined such as the following files:

- The `build.gradle` file is as follows:

```
buildscript {
    ext {
        kotlinVersion = '1.1.60'
        springBootVersion = '2.0.0.M6'
    }
    repositories {
        mavenCentral()
        maven { url "https://repo.spring.io/snapshot" }
        maven { url "https://repo.spring.io/milestone" }
    }
    dependencies {
```

```
            classpath("org.springframework.boot:spring-boot-gradle-
plugin:${springBootVersion}")
            classpath("org.jetbrains.kotlin:kotlin-gradle-
plugin:${kotlinVersion}")
            classpath("org.jetbrains.kotlin:kotlin-
allopen:${kotlinVersion}")
    }
}

apply plugin: 'kotlin'
apply plugin: 'kotlin-spring'
apply plugin: 'eclipse'
apply plugin: 'org.springframework.boot'
apply plugin: 'io.spring.dependency-management'

group = 'com.journaler.config'
version = '0.0.1-SNAPSHOT'
sourceCompatibility = 1.8

compileKotlin {
    kotlinOptions.jvmTarget = "1.8"
}
compileTestKotlin {
    kotlinOptions.jvmTarget = "1.8"
}

repositories {
    mavenCentral()
    maven { url "https://repo.spring.io/snapshot" }
    maven { url "https://repo.spring.io/milestone" }
}

dependencies {
    compile 'org.springframework:spring-context'
    compile 'org.springframework:spring-aop'
    compile 'org.springframework.boot:spring-boot-starter'
    compile 'org.springframework.boot:spring-boot-starter-web'
    compile 'org.springframework.boot:spring-boot-starter-actuator'
    compile 'org.springframework.cloud:spring-cloud-config-server'
    compile 'org.springframework.cloud:spring-cloud-starter-eureka'
    compile 'org.springframework:spring-web'
    compile 'org.springframework:spring-webmvc'
    compile "org.jetbrains.kotlin:kotlin-stdlib-
jre8:${kotlinVersion}"
    compile "org.jetbrains.kotlin:kotlin-reflect:${kotlinVersion}"
    testCompile 'org.springframework.boot:spring-boot-starter-test'
}
```

```
dependencyManagement {
    imports {
        mavenBom "org.springframework.cloud:spring-cloud-
netflix:1.4.1.BUILD-SNAPSHOT"
    }
}
```

- The `application.properties` file is as follows:

```
spring.application.name= config
server.port= 9001
logging.level.root=INFO
logging.level.com.journaler.api=DEBUG
logging.level.org.springframework.jdbc=ERROR

endpoints.health.enabled=true
endpoints.trace.enabled=true
endpoints.info.enabled=true
endpoints.metrics.enabled=true
```

- **Create** `ConfigApplication.kt` **under the** `com.journaler.config` **package:**

```
package com.journaler.config

import org.springframework.boot.SpringApplication
import org.springframework.boot.autoconfigure.SpringBootApplication

@SpringBootApplication
class ConfigApplication

fun main(args: Array<String>) {
    SpringApplication.run(ConfigApplication::class.java, *args)
}
```

Build it and run it. The application will start as a localhost application running on port 9001. As you will remember, our API runs on port 9000.

Let's continue! Update the application class to support Spring Cloud configuration:

```
import org.springframework.cloud.config.server.EnableConfigServer

@SpringBootApplication
@EnableConfigServer
class ConfigApplication

fun main(args: Array<String>) {
    SpringApplication.run(ConfigApplication::class.java, *args)
}
```

Now, extend `application.properties` with the following:

```
spring.cloud.config.server.git.uri=file://${user.home}/Projects/Building-
Applications-with-Spring-5-and-Kotlin-Config-Repo
```

The line we just added defines the location of the Git repository in which we will locate property sources. To have your Git repository ready, navigate into your `home` directory and create a `Projects` directory with a subdirectory named `Building-Applications-with-Spring-5-and-Kotlin-Config-Repo`. To initialize your repository, execute the following:

```
$ git init .
```

The repository is ready. Build and run your application to make sure everything is fine at the moment.

You can clone your existing configuration repository, too! This is an example of some of the lines your `application.properties` requires:

```
spring.cloud.config.server.git.uri=ssh://some_domain/config-repo
spring.cloud.config.server.git.clone-on-start=true
security.user.name=git_username
security.user.password=git_password
```

Discovery

The next thing that we are going to do is provide a mechanism for our servers so that they can discover each other. Eureka discovery server will be the solution for this requirement. We will set up the centralized registry for our applications. The flow will be like this: every one of our servers will contact the discovery server instance and register its address. All others will be able to communicate with it thanks to this.

Set up the new Spring Cloud application, similar to what you did for configuring the application. Make sure it is defined like this:

- The `build.gradle` file configuration:

```
buildscript {
    ext {
        kotlinVersion = '1.1.60'
        springBootVersion = '2.0.0.M6'
    }
    repositories {
        mavenCentral()
```

```
            maven { url "https://repo.spring.io/snapshot" }
            maven { url "https://repo.spring.io/milestone" }
        }
    dependencies {
        classpath("org.springframework.boot:spring-boot-gradle-
plugin:${springBootVersion}")
        classpath("org.jetbrains.kotlin:kotlin-gradle-
plugin:${kotlinVersion}")
        classpath("org.jetbrains.kotlin:kotlin-
allopen:${kotlinVersion}")
    }
}

apply plugin: 'kotlin'
apply plugin: 'kotlin-spring'
apply plugin: 'eclipse'
apply plugin: 'org.springframework.boot'
apply plugin: 'io.spring.dependency-management'

group = 'com.journaler.discovery'
version = '0.0.1-SNAPSHOT'
sourceCompatibility = 1.8

compileKotlin {
    kotlinOptions.jvmTarget = "1.8"
}
compileTestKotlin {
    kotlinOptions.jvmTarget = "1.8"
}

repositories {
    mavenCentral()
    maven { url "https://repo.spring.io/snapshot" }
    maven { url "https://repo.spring.io/milestone" }
}

dependencies {
    compile 'org.springframework:spring-context'
    compile 'org.springframework:spring-aop'
    compile 'org.springframework.boot:spring-boot-starter'
    compile 'org.springframework.boot:spring-boot-starter-web'
    compile 'org.springframework.boot:spring-boot-starter-actuator'
    compile 'org.springframework.cloud:spring-cloud-starter-config'
    compile 'org.springframework.cloud:spring-cloud-starter-eureka-
server'
    compile 'org.springframework:spring-web'
    compile 'org.springframework:spring-webmvc'
    compile "org.jetbrains.kotlin:kotlin-stdlib-
```

```
jre8:${kotlinVersion}"
    compile "org.jetbrains.kotlin:kotlin-reflect:${kotlinVersion}"
    testCompile 'org.springframework.boot:spring-boot-starter-test'
}

dependencyManagement {
    imports {
        mavenBom "org.springframework.cloud:spring-cloud-
netflix:1.4.1.BUILD-SNAPSHOT"
    }
}
```

The most important dependencies which have been introduced to us include the following:

```
compile 'org.springframework.cloud:spring-cloud-starter-config'
compile 'org.springframework.cloud:spring-cloud-starter-eureka-server'
mavenBom "org.springframework.cloud:spring-cloud-netflix:1.4.1.BUILD-
SNAPSHOT"
```

Instead of having the traditional `application.properties` file in the application resources, we will define the `bootstrap.properties` file that will define which configuration server to target, the port for it, and the configuration name:

```
spring.cloud.config.name=discovery
spring.cloud.config.uri=http://localhost:9001
```

The last thing we need is the `Application` class, defining `DiscoveryApplication.kt` with the following content:

```
package com.journaler.discovery

import org.springframework.boot.SpringApplication
import org.springframework.boot.autoconfigure.SpringBootApplication
import org.springframework.cloud.netflix.eureka.server.EnableEurekaServer

@SpringBootApplication
@EnableEurekaServer
class DiscoveryApplication

fun main(args: Array<String>) {
    SpringApplication.run(DiscoveryApplication::class.java, *args)
}
```

As you can see, all we have to do is to enable the Eureka server by adding the @EnableEurekaServer annotation.

Before we run anything, create a configuration file in your Git repository named discovery.properties (the file we create must have the same name as the spring.application.name property value):

```
spring.application.name= discovery
server.port= 9002
logging.level.root=INFO
logging.level.com.journaler.api=DEBUG
logging.level.org.springframework.jdbc=ERROR

endpoints.health.enabled=true
endpoints.trace.enabled=true
endpoints.info.enabled=true
endpoints.metrics.enabled=true

eureka.instance.hostname=localhost

eureka.client.serviceUrl.defaultZone=http://localhost:9002/eureka/
eureka.client.register-with-eureka=false
eureka.client.fetch-registry=false
```

What does this configuration represent? First of all, it contains the standard information we usually provide. Additionally, there is the following:

```
eureka.instance.hostname=localhost
eureka.client.serviceUrl.defaultZone=http://localhost:9002/eureka/
eureka.client.register-with-eureka=false
eureka.client.fetch-registry=false
```

With this, we are telling the server that it's operating in the default zone, which means that we are matching the configuration client's region setting. It's important to note that we are also defining the behavior which the server does not do with any another discovery instance!

Now, save all your work, build and run the configuration server first, and then the discovery server second. If you look at your log for the discovery application, you will notice that this is working:

- The upper part of the printed log:

```
[             main] s.b.c.e.t.TomcatEmbeddedServletContainer : Tomcat initialized with port(s): 9002 (http)
[             main] o.apache.catalina.core.StandardService   : Starting service [Tomcat]
[             main] org.apache.catalina.core.StandardEngine  : Starting Servlet Engine: Apache Tomcat/8.5.23
[ost-startStop-1] o.a.c.c.C.[Tomcat].[localhost].[/]        : Initializing Spring embedded WebApplicationContext
[ost-startStop-1] o.s.web.context.ContextLoader             : Root WebApplicationContext: initialization completed in 1028 ms
```

- The lower part of the printed log:

```
[        Thread-24] e.s.EurekaServerInitializerConfiguration : Started Eureka Server
[             main] s.b.c.e.t.TomcatEmbeddedServletContainer : Tomcat started on port(s): 9002 (http)
[             main] .s.c.n.e.s.EurekaAutoServiceRegistration  : Updating port to 9002
[             main] c.j.discovery.DiscoveryApplicationKt      : Started DiscoveryApplicationKt in 6.34 seconds (JVM running for 7.012)
[192.168.100.188] c.c.c.ConfigServicePropertySourceLocator  : Fetching config from server at: http://localhost:9001
[192.168.100.188] c.c.c.ConfigServicePropertySourceLocator  : Located environment: name=discovery, profiles=[default], label=null,
[a-EvictionTimer] c.n.e.registry.AbstractInstanceRegistry   : Running the evict task with compensationTime 0ms
[a-EvictionTimer] c.n.e.registry.AbstractInstanceRegistry   : Running the evict task with compensationTime 0ms
```

Gateway

The next step in our distributed system is defining the gateway. The gateway is used to allow all responses to originate from a single host. Let's create another Spring Cloud application. Make sure it's defined as in the following files:

- The `build.gradle` file is as follows:

```
buildscript {
    ext {
        kotlinVersion = '1.1.60'
        springBootVersion = '2.0.0.M6'
    }
    repositories {
        mavenCentral()
        maven { url "https://repo.spring.io/snapshot" }
        maven { url "https://repo.spring.io/milestone" }
    }
    dependencies {
        classpath("org.springframework.boot:spring-boot-gradle-
plugin:${springBootVersion}")
        classpath("org.jetbrains.kotlin:kotlin-gradle-
plugin:${kotlinVersion}")
        classpath("org.jetbrains.kotlin:kotlin-
```

```
allopen:${kotlinVersion}")
    }
}

apply plugin: 'kotlin'
apply plugin: 'kotlin-spring'
apply plugin: 'eclipse'
apply plugin: 'org.springframework.boot'
apply plugin: 'io.spring.dependency-management'

group = 'com.journaler.gateway'
version = '0.0.1-SNAPSHOT'
sourceCompatibility = 1.8

compileKotlin {
    kotlinOptions.jvmTarget = "1.8"
}
compileTestKotlin {
    kotlinOptions.jvmTarget = "1.8"
}

repositories {
    mavenCentral()
    maven { url "https://repo.spring.io/snapshot" }
    maven { url "https://repo.spring.io/milestone" }
}

dependencies {
    compile 'org.springframework:spring-context'
    compile 'org.springframework:spring-aop'
    compile 'org.springframework.boot:spring-boot-starter'
    compile 'org.springframework.boot:spring-boot-starter-web'
    compile 'org.springframework.boot:spring-boot-starter-actuator'
    compile 'org.springframework.cloud:spring-cloud-starter-config'
    compile 'org.springframework.cloud:spring-cloud-starter-eureka-
server'
    compile 'org.springframework.cloud:spring-cloud-starter-zuul'
    compile 'org.springframework:spring-web'
    compile 'org.springframework:spring-webmvc'
    compile "org.jetbrains.kotlin:kotlin-stdlib-
jre8:${kotlinVersion}"
    compile "org.jetbrains.kotlin:kotlin-reflect:${kotlinVersion}"
    testCompile 'org.springframework.boot:spring-boot-starter-test'
}

dependencyManagement {
    imports {
        mavenBom "org.springframework.cloud:spring-cloud-
```

```
netflix:1.4.1.BUILD-SNAPSHOT"
    }
}
```

- The `bootstrap.properties` file is as follows:

```
spring.cloud.config.name=gateway
spring.cloud.config.discovery.service-id=config
spring.cloud.config.discovery.enabled=true
eureka.client.serviceUrl.defaultZone=http://localhost:9002/eureka/
```

- Under the `com.journaler.gateway` package, create the `Application` class:

```
package com.journaler.gateway

import org.springframework.boot.SpringApplication
import org.springframework.boot.autoconfigure.SpringBootApplication
import org.springframework.cloud.netflix.eureka.EnableEurekaClient
import org.springframework.cloud.netflix.zuul.EnableZuulProxy

@SpringBootApplication
@EnableZuulProxy
@EnableEurekaClient
class GatewayApplication

fun main(args: Array<String>) {
    SpringApplication.run(GatewayApplication::class.java, *args)
}
```

Then, update `application.properties` for the configuration server application by adding these lines:

```
eureka.client.region = default
eureka.client.registryFetchIntervalSeconds = 5
eureka.client.serviceUrl.defaultZone=http://localhost:9002/eureka/
```

This will allow us to establish a communication between the configuration and discovery servers so that we can finalize this part of the implementation.

So, what did we just do? Let's go through it. First of all, we satisfied the necessary dependencies to use Spring Cloud as a proxy for our needs by adding the following:

```
compile 'org.springframework.cloud:spring-cloud-starter-config'
compile 'org.springframework.cloud:spring-cloud-starter-eureka-server'
compile 'org.springframework.cloud:spring-cloud-starter-zuul'

mavenBom "org.springframework.cloud:spring-cloud-netflix:1.4.1.BUILD-
SNAPSHOT"
```

Then, we defined the gateway application as the configuration and discovery client and gateway proxy. We achieved this by using `@EnableEurekaClient` and `@EnableZuulProxy` annotations.

The most important part comes with the properties definition. The `bootstrap.properties` configuration tells our application to talk to the discovery server to obtain its configuration. The rest of the configuration is defined under our Git repository. The `zuul.routes` property has the purpose of routing requests based on a URL matcher. We tell Zuul to route any request that comes in on the `'/journaler/**'` path to the application with the `spring.application.name` property of `journaler`. Zuul will then perform a lookup. The host from the discovery server using the application name will be found and the request will be forwarded to it.

Finally, we will run all of the applications. Start the configuration and discovery servers (applications). Then, run the gateway application. Observe that in your logs, you will have something similar to this:

- The upper part of the log:

```
[       main] c.c.c.ConfigServicePropertySourceLocator : Fetching config from server at: http://192.168.100.188:9001/
[       main] c.c.c.ConfigServicePropertySourceLocator : Located environment: name=gateway, profiles=[default], label=null,
[       main] b.c.PropertySourceBootstrapConfiguration : Located property source: CompositePropertySource [name='configService'
[       main] c.j.gateway.GatewayApplicationKt         : No active profile set, falling back to default profiles: default
[       main] ationConfigEmbeddedWebApplicationContext : Refreshing org.springframework.boot.context.embedded.AnnotationConfig
[       main] o.s.b.f.s.DefaultListableBeanFactory     : Overriding bean definition for bean 'counterFactory' with a different
[       main] o.s.cloud.context.scope.GenericScope     : BeanFactory id=45009661-8d31-3b79-818f-99c11e40370e
[       main] f.a.AutowiredAnnotationBeanPostProcessor : JSR-330 'javax.inject.Inject' annotation found and supported for auto
[       main] trationDelegate$BeanPostProcessorChecker : Bean 'org.springframework.cloud.netflix.metrics.MetricsInterceptorConf
[       main] trationDelegate$BeanPostProcessorChecker : Bean 'org.springframework.cloud.autoconfigure.ConfigurationProperties
[       main] s.b.c.e.t.TomcatEmbeddedServletContainer : Tomcat initialized with port(s): 9003 (http)
[       main] o.apache.catalina.core.StandardService   : Starting service [Tomcat]
[       main] org.apache.catalina.core.StandardEngine  : Starting Servlet Engine: Apache Tomcat/8.5.23
[ost-startStop-1] o.a.c.c.C.[Tomcat].[localhost].[/]    : Initializing Spring embedded WebApplicationContext
[ost-startStop-1] o.s.web.context.ContextLoader         : Root WebApplicationContext: initialization completed in 1518 ms
```

- The lower part of the log:

```
[        main] com.netflix.discovery.DiscoveryClient      : Getting all instance registry info from the eureka server
[        main] com.netflix.discovery.DiscoveryClient      : The response status is 200
[        main] com.netflix.discovery.DiscoveryClient      : Starting heartbeat executor: renew interval is: 30
[        main] c.n.discovery.InstanceInfoReplicator        : InstanceInfoReplicator onDemand update allowed rate per min is 4
[        main] com.netflix.discovery.DiscoveryClient      : Discovery Client initialized at timestamp 1514903513512 with initial instances count:
[        main] o.s.c.n.e.s.EurekaServiceRegistry           : Registering application gateway with eureka with status UP
[        main] com.netflix.discovery.DiscoveryClient      : Saw local status change event StatusChangeEvent [timestamp=1514903513548, current=UP,
[nfoReplicator-0] com.netflix.discovery.DiscoveryClient   : DiscoveryClient_GATEWAY/192.168.100.188:gateway:9003: registering service...
[nfoReplicator-0] com.netflix.discovery.DiscoveryClient   : DiscoveryClient_GATEWAY/192.168.100.188:gateway:9003 - registration status: 204
[        main] o.s.c.support.DefaultLifecycleProcessor     : Starting beans in phase 2147483647
[        main] ration$HystrixMetricsPollerConfiguration    : Starting poller
[        main] s.b.c.e.t.TomcatEmbeddedServletContainer    : Tomcat started on port(s): 9003 (http)
[        main] .s.c.n.e.s.EurekaAutoServiceRegistration    : Updating port to 9003
[        main] c.j.gateway.GatewayApplicationKt            : Started GatewayApplicationKt in 8.884 seconds (JVM running for 9.583)
[192.168.100.188] c.c.c.ConfigServicePropertySourceLocator : Fetching config from server at: http://192.168.100.188:9001/
[192.168.100.188] c.c.c.ConfigServicePropertySourceLocator : Located environment: name=gateway, profiles=[default], label=null, version=082b318403
```

Updating the API application

The Journaler API application hasn't been updated to be part of the distributed configuration system, yet. We will reconfigure it now! It doesn't require too much work to achieve this. The first thing we will do is update our dependencies. Open the `build.gradle` configuration and make sure your dependencies are as follows:

```
...
dependencies {
    ...
    compile 'org.springframework.cloud:spring-cloud-starter-config'
    compile 'org.springframework.cloud:spring-cloud-starter-eureka'
    ...
}

dependencyManagement {
    imports {
        mavenBom "org.springframework.cloud:spring-cloud-netflix:1.4.1.BUILD-SNAPSHOT"
    }
}
```

When the dependencies are satisfied, we can update our `Application` class. Open the `ApiApplication` class and modify it by adding the proper annotations so that the application is a Eureka server client:

```
package com.journaler.api

import org.springframework.boot.SpringApplication
import org.springframework.boot.autoconfigure.SpringBootApplication
import org.springframework.cloud.netflix.eureka.EnableEurekaClient
```

```
@SpringBootApplication
@EnableEurekaClient
class ApiApplication

fun main(args: Array<String>) {
    SpringApplication.run(ApiApplication::class.java, *args)
}
```

In the Git repository, create a `journaler.properties` configuration file:

```
spring.application.name= journaler
server.port= 9000
logging.level.root=INFO
logging.level.com.journaler.api=DEBUG
logging.level.org.springframework.jdbc=ERROR

endpoints.health.enabled=true
endpoints.trace.enabled=true
endpoints.info.enabled=true
endpoints.metrics.enabled=true

spring.datasource.url=
jdbc:mysql://localhost/journaler_api?useSSL=false&useUnicode=true&character
Encoding=utf-8

spring.datasource.username=root
spring.datasource.password=localInstance2017
spring.datasource.tomcat.test-on-borrow=true
spring.datasource.tomcat.validation-interval=30000
spring.datasource.tomcat.validation-query=SELECT 1
spring.datasource.tomcat.remove-abandoned=true
spring.datasource.tomcat.remove-abandoned-timeout=10000
spring.datasource.tomcat.log-abandoned=true
spring.datasource.tomcat.max-age=1800000
spring.datasource.tomcat.log-validation-errors=true
spring.datasource.tomcat.max-active=50
spring.datasource.tomcat.max-idle=10

spring.jpa.hibernate.ddl-auto=update

eureka.client.region = default
eureka.client.registryFetchIntervalSeconds = 5
eureka.client.serviceUrl.defaultZone=http://localhost:9002/eureka/
```

And finally, remove `application.properties` from the resources directory. Instead, create a `bootstrap.properties` file with the following configuration:

```
spring.cloud.config.name=journaler
spring.cloud.config.discovery.service-id=config
spring.cloud.config.discovery.enabled=true

eureka.client.serviceUrl.defaultZone=http://localhost:9002/eureka/
```

Now, we are ready to run and try everything! Start all of the applications one by one:

- Configuration
- Discovery
- Gateway
- Journaler API application

Observe the Journaler API logs. You will have a log output similar to this:

- The upper part of the log:

```
[         main] c.c.c.ConfigServicePropertySourceLocator : Fetching config from server at: http://192.168.0.14:9001/
[         main] c.c.c.ConfigServicePropertySourceLocator : Located environment: name=journaler, profiles=[default],
[         main] b.c.PropertySourceBootstrapConfiguration : Located property source: CompositePropertySource [name='
[         main] com.journaler.api.ApiApplicationKt       : No active profile set, falling back to default profiles:
[         main] ationConfigEmbeddedWebApplicationContext : Refreshing org.springframework.boot.context.embedded.Annot
[         main] o.s.cloud.context.scope.GenericScope     : BeanFactory id=0b693855-5db9-3065-8dc4-598527e3466c
[         main] f.a.AutowiredAnnotationBeanPostProcessor : JSR-330 'javax.inject.Inject' annotation found and support
[         main] trationDelegate$BeanPostProcessorChecker : Bean 'org.springframework.transaction.annotation.ProxyTrans
[         main] trationDelegate$BeanPostProcessorChecker : Bean 'org.springframework.cloud.netflix.metrics.MetricsInt
[         main] trationDelegate$BeanPostProcessorChecker : Bean 'org.springframework.cloud.autoconfigure.Configuration
[         main] s.b.c.e.t.TomcatEmbeddedServletContainer : Tomcat initialized with port(s): 9000 (http)
[         main] o.apache.catalina.core.StandardService   : Starting service [Tomcat]
[         main] org.apache.catalina.core.StandardEngine  : Starting Servlet Engine: Apache Tomcat/8.5.23
```

- The lower part of the log:

```
[         main] o.s.c.n.e.s.EurekaServiceRegistry        : Registering application journaler with eureka with status UP
[         main] com.netflix.discovery.DiscoveryClient    : Saw local status change event StatusChangeEvent [timestamp=1514989767517, curren
[nfoReplicator-0] com.netflix.discovery.DiscoveryClient  : DiscoveryClient_JOURNALER/192.168.0.14:journaler:9000: registering service...
[nfoReplicator-0] com.netflix.discovery.DiscoveryClient  : DiscoveryClient_JOURNALER/192.168.0.14:journaler:9000 - registration status: 204
[         main] s.b.c.e.t.TomcatEmbeddedServletContainer : Tomcat started on port(s): 9000 (http)
[         main] .s.c.n.e.s.EurekaAutoServiceRegistration : Updating port to 9000
[         main] com.journaler.api.ApiApplicationKt       : Started ApiApplicationKt in 9.909 seconds (JVM running for 10.352)
```

When the Journaler API application is started, try some existing API calls:

- [**POST**] `http://localhost:9000/login`. The result is as follows:

- [**GET**] `http://localhost:9000/notes`. The result is as follows:

The GET API call for notes

Now, try the same API calls through the gateway server running on port 9003:

- [**POST**] http://localhost:9003/journaler/login. The result is as follows:

The POST API call for login through the gateway server

- [**GET**] http://localhost:9003/journaler/notes. The result is as follows:

The GET API call for notes through the gateway server

As you can see, the **GET** method for notes executed through the gateway server (application) returns an unauthorized response to us. This is because the application is not aware of the session we obtained. To be able for this to work, we must set up session sharing for that purpose. Sharing sessions gives us the ability to log in users of the system on our Gateway application and then propagate authentication to other services that depend on it.

Securing Spring Cloud services

In this section, we will secure our Spring Cloud configuration and for simplicity purposes, temporarily free the Journaler API from security limits. We will demonstrate the basic principles of securing microservices and guide you step by step in achieving this.

Each of our modules must support Spring Security and Spring sessions. For that purpose, extend each `build.gradle` configuration with Spring Security and Spring session support dependencies:

```
...
dependencies {
    compile 'org.springframework.boot:spring-boot-starter-security'
}
...
```

We will store all of our sessions in memory. For that purpose, we will use the Redis in-memory database. We have to extend each of our applications to support it by extending `build.gradle` with the following dependency:

```
...
dependencies {
    compile 'org.springframework.boot:spring-boot-starter-data-redis'
}
...
```

Now, we are ready to add session configuration. Add the session configuration class in the same package level where the main application class is defined:

```
package com.journaler.api

import
org.springframework.session.data.redis.config.annotation.web.http.EnableRed
isHttpSession
import
org.springframework.session.web.context.AbstractHttpSessionApplicationIniti
alizer

@EnableRedisHttpSession
class SessionConfiguration : AbstractHttpSessionApplicationInitializer()
```

Do the same for the following applications: discovery, gateway, and Journaler API. You will have three classes with the same implementation! After you are finished with the session configuration class, extend your application configurations defined in your Git repository (for all three applications) by adding the following code:

```
spring.redis.host=localhost
spring.redis.port=6379
```

This will provide proper Redis configuration for each application.

For the `Configuration` application, extend its `application.properties` with the following:

```
eureka.client.region = default
eureka.client.registryFetchIntervalSeconds = 5

eureka.client.serviceUrl.defaultZone=
http://discoveryAdmin:discoveryPassword12345@localhost:9002/eureka/

security.user.name=configAdmin
security.user.password=configPassword12345
security.user.role=SYSTEM

spring.session.store-type=redis
```

By doing this, we will make sure that the application logs in with discovery. We must secure the discovery service, too. Create package security with the `WebSecurityConfiguration` class defined like this:

```
package com.journaler.discovery.security

import
org.springframework.security.config.annotation.web.builders.HttpSecurity
import
org.springframework.security.config.annotation.authentication.builders.Auth
enticationManagerBuilder
import org.springframework.beans.factory.annotation.Autowired
import org.springframework.context.annotation.Configuration
import org.springframework.core.annotation.Order
import
org.springframework.security.config.annotation.web.configuration.WebSecurit
yConfigurerAdapter
import
org.springframework.security.config.annotation.web.configuration.EnableWebS
ecurity
import org.springframework.security.config.http.SessionCreationPolicy


@Configuration
@EnableWebSecurity
@Order(1)
class SecurityConfig : WebSecurityConfigurerAdapter() {

    @Autowired
    fun configureGlobal(auth: AuthenticationManagerBuilder) {
        auth
                .inMemoryAuthentication()
```

```
                .withUser("discoveryAdmin")
                .password("discoveryPassword12345")
                .roles("SYSTEM")
    }

    override fun configure(http: HttpSecurity) {
        http
                .sessionManagement()
                .sessionCreationPolicy(SessionCreationPolicy.ALWAYS)
                .and().requestMatchers().antMatchers("/eureka/**")
                .and().authorizeRequests().antMatchers("/eureka/**")
                .hasRole("SYSTEM").anyRequest().denyAll().and()
                .httpBasic().and().csrf().disable()
    }
}
```

This will match the username and password combination from the `Configuration` application properties. We must note that we used the `@Order` annotation so that we can tell Spring to use this configuration as its first priority. With the `sessionCreationPolicy()` method and `ALWAYS` parameter, we defined that the session will be created on every user login attempt.

The next thing we are going to do is tell the discovery application about the credentials to use for logging in the configuration application. Extend its `bootstrap.properties` configuration so that it look like this:

```
spring.cloud.config.name=discovery
spring.cloud.config.uri=http://localhost:9001
spring.cloud.config.username=configAdmin
spring.cloud.config.password=configPassword12345
```

Finally, modify the `discovery.properties` configuration from our Git repository:

```
...
eureka.client.serviceUrl.defaultZone=
http://discoveryAdmin:discoveryPassword12345@localhost:9002/eureka/
eureka.client.register-with-eureka=false
eureka.client.fetch-registry=false
...
```

We extended the configuration with the credentials for our discovery application.

Since we've secured the configuration and discovery applications, it's time to do the same for our gateway application. Create a `security` package containing the `WebSecurityConfiguration` class:

```
package com.journaler.gateway.security

import
org.springframework.security.config.annotation.web.builders.HttpSecurity
import
org.springframework.security.config.annotation.authentication.builders.Auth
enticationManagerBuilder
import org.springframework.beans.factory.annotation.Autowired
import org.springframework.context.annotation.Configuration
import org.springframework.core.annotation.Order
import
org.springframework.security.config.annotation.web.configuration.WebSecurit
yConfigurerAdapter
import
org.springframework.security.config.annotation.web.configuration.EnableWebS
ecurity

@Configuration
@EnableWebSecurity
@Order(1)
class SecurityConfig : WebSecurityConfigurerAdapter() {

    @Autowired
    fun configureGlobal(auth: AuthenticationManagerBuilder) {
        auth
                .inMemoryAuthentication()
                .withUser("user")
                .password("12345")
                .roles("USER")
                .and()
                .withUser("admin")
                .password("12345")
                .roles("ADMIN")
    }

    override fun configure(http: HttpSecurity) {
        http
                .authorizeRequests()
                .antMatchers("/journaler/**")
                .permitAll()
                .antMatchers("/eureka/**").hasRole("ADMIN")
                .anyRequest().authenticated()
                .and()
```

```
                    .formLogin()
                    .and()
                    .logout().permitAll()
                    .logoutSuccessUrl("/journaler/**").permitAll()
                    .and()
                    .csrf().disable()
        }
    }
```

We have defined two users with two roles: the regular user and the admin user. We also defined the security filter with form login. Now, switch to gateway's session configuration class and update it:

```
package com.journaler.gateway

import org.springframework.session.data.redis.RedisFlushMode
import
org.springframework.session.data.redis.config.annotation.web.http.EnableRed
isHttpSession
import
org.springframework.session.web.context.AbstractHttpSessionApplicationIniti
alizer

@EnableRedisHttpSession(redisFlushMode = RedisFlushMode.IMMEDIATE)
class SessionConfiguration : AbstractHttpSessionApplicationInitializer()
```

Any changes that have occurred on the session will be persisted immediately! Finally, we will add functionality so that we can forward an authentication token after login. Create a new class called `SessionFilter`:

```
package com.journaler.gateway

import com.netflix.zuul.ZuulFilter
import com.netflix.zuul.context.RequestContext
import org.springframework.stereotype.Component
import org.springframework.session.SessionRepository
import org.springframework.beans.factory.annotation.Autowired

@Component
class SessionFilter : ZuulFilter() {

    @Autowired
    lateinit var repository: SessionRepository<*>

    override fun shouldFilter(): Boolean {
        return true
    }
```

```kotlin
    override fun run(): Any? {
        val context = RequestContext.getCurrentContext()
        val httpSession = context.request.session
        val session = repository?.getSession(httpSession.id)
        context.addZuulRequestHeader("Cookie", "SESSION=" + httpSession.id)
        println("Session ID available: ${session.id}")
        return null
    }

    override fun filterType(): String {
        return "pre"
    }

    override fun filterOrder(): Int {
        return 0
    }
}
```

The filter we just defined will take a request and add the session key as a cookie in the request's header.

Before we update our Journaler API application, we need to make a few small updates. Update the `bootstrap.properties` configuration:

```
spring.cloud.config.name=gateway
spring.cloud.config.discovery.service-id=config
spring.cloud.config.discovery.enabled=true
spring.cloud.config.username=configAdmin
spring.cloud.config.password=configPassword12345
eureka.client.serviceUrl.defaultZone=
http://discoveryAdmin:discoveryPassword12345@localhost:9002/eureka/
```

Also, update `gateway.properties` in our Git repository:

```
spring.application.name=gateway
server.port=9003

eureka.client.region = default
eureka.client.registryFetchIntervalSeconds = 5

management.security.sessions=always
```

```
spring.redis.host=localhost
spring.redis.port=6379

zuul.routes.journaler.path=/journaler/**
zuul.routes.journaler.sensitive-headers=Set-Cookie,Authorization
hystrix.command.journaler.execution.isolation.thread.timeoutInMilliseconds=
600000

zuul.routes.discovery.path=/discovery/**
zuul.routes.discovery.sensitive-headers=Set-Cookie,Authorization
zuul.routes.discovery.url=http://localhost:9002
hystrix.command.discovery.execution.isolation.thread.timeoutInMilliseconds=
600000
```

We defined that session management will always generate sessions. We also moved configuration for Redis so that it is defined after session management.

We can remove the `serviceUrl.defaultZone` property from the `gateway.properties` file to our configuration Git repository. This value is duplicated in the bootstrap file.

Commit all Git repositories that have configuration changes so that these changes take effect in our next run!

We are very close to completing our final touches on the Journaler API! Before we do this, let's run the configuration, discovery, and gateway applications. To be able to run them, we will install the Redis server. We will use Homebrew on macOS for the installation process. It's very simple and easy. Open your Terminal and execute the following:

```
$ brew install redis
```

After some time, Redis will be installed. Now, start it by issuing the following command:

```
$ redis-server
```

The Redis server will start:

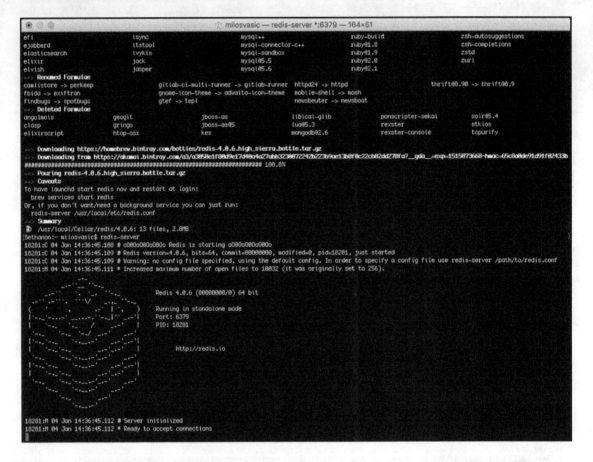

For any other OS, please follow instructions from the official Redis homepage: `https://redis.io/`.

Now, run the configuration, discovery, and gateway applications one by one. Everything should work properly!

Open the `WebSecurityConfiguration` class from the Journaler API application and change it. The new implementation should look like this:

```
package com.journaler.api.security

import org.springframework.context.annotation.Configuration
import
org.springframework.security.config.annotation.web.configuration.EnableWebS
```

```
ecurity
import
org.springframework.security.config.annotation.web.configuration.WebSecurit
yConfigurerAdapter
import
org.springframework.security.config.annotation.web.builders.HttpSecurity
import org.springframework.core.annotation.Order

@Configuration
@EnableWebSecurity
@Order(1)
class SecurityConfig : WebSecurityConfigurerAdapter() {

    override fun configure(http: HttpSecurity) {
        http
                .httpBasic().disable().authorizeRequests()
                .antMatchers("/notes").permitAll()
                .antMatchers("/notes/**").permitAll()
                .antMatchers("/todos").permitAll()
                .antMatchers("/todos/**").permitAll()
                .anyRequest()
                .authenticated()
                .and()
                .csrf().disable()
    }
}
```

Please, remove all user entity-related classes and others security-related classes that are not in use anymore!

Now, update the `bootstrap.properties` configuration:

```
spring.cloud.config.name=journaler
spring.cloud.config.discovery.service-id=config
spring.cloud.config.discovery.enabled=true

spring.cloud.config.username=configAdmin
spring.cloud.config.password=configPassword12345
eureka.client.serviceUrl.defaultZone=
http://discoveryAdmin:discoveryPassword12345@localhost:9002/eureka/
```

Update and commit the `journaler.properties` file in our Git repository:

```
...
management.security.sessions=never
...
```

We also removed the `serviceUrl.defaultZone` property since it's already defined in the `boots.properties` configuration.

Since we were updating our dependencies during development, we didn't notice that we now have a problem with request classes and DTOs. We must introduce a default empty constructor for each one. Let's do this quickly:

- NoteDTO:

```
data class NoteDTO(
        var title: String,
        var message: String,
        var location: String = ""
) {
    constructor() : this("", "", "")
    ...
}
```

- TodoDTO:

```
data class TodoDTO(
        var title: String,
        var message: String,
        var schedule: Long,
        var location: String = ""
) {
    ...
    constructor() : this("", "", -1, "")
}
```

- NoteFindByTitleRequest:

```
package com.journaler.api.controller

data class NoteFindByTitleRequest(val title: String) {

    constructor() : this("")

}
```

- TodoLaterThanRequest:

```
package com.journaler.api.controller

import java.util.*

data class TodoLaterThanRequest(val date: Date? = null) {
```

```
        constructor() : this(null)

    }
```

- TodoService:

```
@Service("Todo service")
class TodoService {
    ...
    fun getScheduledLaterThan(date: Date?): Iterable<TodoDTO> {
        date?.let {
            return repository.findScheduledLaterThan(date.time).map
{ it -> TodoDTO(it) }
        }
        return listOf()
    }
}
```

If you need to remove all of the tables from the database, then run the Journaler API application. Let's try a couple of calls that are targeting the gateway application and confirm that all calls are redirected:

- [**PUT**] http://localhost:9003/journaler/notes: Execute the call a couple of times:

- [**GET**] `http://localhost:9003/journaler/notes`:

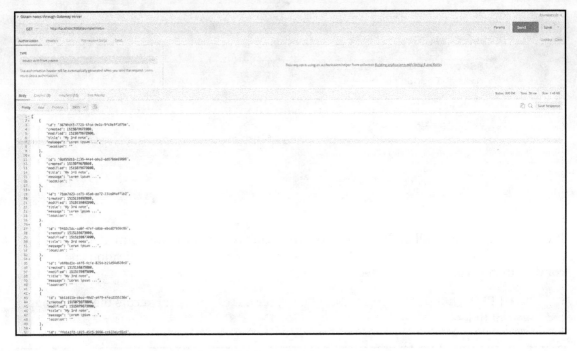

The GET API call for notes through the gateway application

- [**POST**] `http://localhost:9003/journaler/notes/by_title` with the title parameter `"My 1st note"`:

- [**POST**] `http://localhost:9003/journaler/notes/by_title` with the title parameter `"My 3rd note"`:

The POST API call for notes through the gateway application

Summary

Spring Cloud is a very powerful framework! Even though we went on a long journey in this chapter, we only touched on the basics of Spring Cloud. It's important that you understand what it is possible to achieve and how to start doing so. If you think this was too complex, please start over from the beginning of this chapter and do all of the exercises slowly. If you understood all of this, then the next thing you should do is make it possible for Spring sessions to be propagated to the Journaler API and make use of it with the full Spring Security configuration we removed at the end of our exercises. Take your time and do as much researching and coding as you can! In the next chapter, we will look at Project Reactor and try to demonstrate how and why you should go reactive!

7
Using Project Reactor

In this chapter, we will demonstrate how to use Spring with Project Reactor. Project Reactor is a project that provides us with event-based architecture. With Project Reactor, we can asynchronously handle a large volume of concurrent service requests. Project Reactor is known as the guardian of latency and offers non-blocking and backpressure-ready embeddable solutions.

Here, we will explain the following:

- Why you should use Project Reactor
- What Project Reactor is
- How to make RESTful calls reactive

Why use Project Reactor?

There are a lot of good reasons for our project to support Project Reactor. If you plan to develop serious enterprise software, Project Reactor will most likely offer solutions for some of the most common challenges. Let's have a brief look at its power features:

- It is fully non-blocking
- It offers reactive API such as `Flux [N]` and `Mono [0|1]`, each implementing Reactive Extension (http://reactivex.io/)
- It is suited to the microservices architecture
- It supports backpressure-ready network engines
- It is efficient at passing messages

In the next sections of this chapter, we will give you a further explanation of Project Reactor and how it can be used with Spring. We will demonstrate its use by extending our code base to support Project Reactor.

What is Project Reactor?

Project Reactor is a project divided into several sub-projects. Each has a different purpose which combined, makes, a first-class tool for modern application development. Project Reactor consists of the following components:

- **Reactor Core**: Core components
- **Reactor Test**: Collection of test utilities
- **Reactor Adapter**: For adapting to (or from) other reactive libraries
- **Reactor Netty**: For developing HTTP, TCP, UDP client/servers with Netty
- **Reactor Extra**: Additional operators for Flux
- **Reactor Kafka**: Reactive bridge to Apache Kafka
- **Reactor RabbitMQ**: Reactive bridge to RabbitMQ
- **Reactor Core .NET**: Reactive Streams foundation for .NET
- **Reactor Core JS**: Reactive Streams foundation for JavaScript

In the next section, we will adapt our API to use Project Reactor and improve our existing code base. Unfortunately, we will not be able to cover all Project Reactor sub-projects but we will give you an idea of how Project Reactor can be utilized. For more information about Project Reactor, you can take a look at the official documentation since the project is well documented!

Using Project Reactor

It is time to update our REST API so that it becomes an event-driven application. You will see that the changes we make are not difficult to apply. We will start by updating our dependencies so that Project Reactor classes are accessible. Open your API application `build.gradle` configuration and extend it:

```
...
dependencies {
    ...
    compile 'io.projectreactor:reactor-bus:2.0.8.RELEASE'
    ...
}
...
```

Here, we introduced support for a Project Reactor bus. We will use it to trigger an action in some particular situations. We will email the system administrator if the number of total Notes or TODOs in the system reaches a critical level. This example is trivial. One good example would be triggering actions when storage reaches a significant number of sold items. Another could be if the number of unsubscribed users increases more than a certain percentage, and so on.

We will define some simple entity to represent the notification. Create a package called `reactor` under the `data` package with the data class member `NotesCountNotification`:

```
package com.journaler.api.reactor

data class NotesCountNotification(val notesCount: Int)

Create almost the same class for TODO notification data:
package com.journaler.api.reactor

data class TodosCountNotification(val todosCount: Int)
```

We need service abstraction for both data classes. Under the `reactor` package, create a member interface `NotificationService`:

```
package com.journaler.api.reactor

interface NotificationService<in T> {

    fun notify(notification: T)

}
```

The note and TODO notification service interfaces for the entity count will look like the following:

- `NotesCountNotificationService`:

```
package com.journaler.api.reactor

import org.springframework.stereotype.Service


interface NotesCountNotificationService :
NotificationService<NotesCountNotification>
```

- TodosCountNotificationService:

```
package com.journaler.api.reactor

import org.springframework.stereotype.Service


interface TodosCountNotificationService :
NotificationService<TodosCountNotification>
```

For each main interface, we must have the proper implementation. Since we will be sending email messages, we must add Spring email dependency. Extend the `build.gradle` configuration with the following:

```
...
dependencies {
    ...
    compile 'org.springframework.boot:spring-boot-starter-mail'
    ...
}
```

To be able to send email messages, we must satisfy some requirements. We must have several classes ready so it is possible to send emails. We will create them one, by one but first create a new package called `mail` and then the first class called `MailMessage`:

```
package com.journaler.api.mail
import org.hibernate.validator.constraints.Email
import org.jetbrains.annotations.NotNull
data class MailMessage
(
@Email
@NotNull
val to: String,
val subject: String,
val text: String
)
```

We defined base entity to represent the message that we will send. We want to be able to send email messages without any attachment. For that purpose, we will create an interface to represent the functionality, called `EmailService`:

```
package com.journaler.api.mail
interface MailService {
    fun sendMessage(message: MailMessage)
}
```

The implementation should look like the following (`MailServiceImpl.kt`):

```
package com.journaler.api.mail

import org.springframework.beans.factory.annotation.Autowired
import org.springframework.mail.SimpleMailMessage
import org.springframework.mail.javamail.JavaMailSender
import org.springframework.stereotype.Component

@Component
class MailServiceImpl : MailService {

    @Autowired
    lateinit var sender: JavaMailSender

    override fun sendMessage(message: MailMessage) {
        val toSend = SimpleMailMessage()
        toSend.to = arrayOf(message.to)
        toSend.subject = message.subject
        toSend.text = message.text
        sender.send(toSend)
    }

}
```

As you can see in the preceding code, we defined Spring Component and injected a dependency for `JavaMailSender` implementation: `JavaMailSenderImpl`. This class is responsible for executing the mail sending operation. We are almost ready to be able to send email messages. There is one last thing left to do. We must provide email server configuration. Open `journaler.configuration` from our configuration Git repository and provide parameters, as in the following example:

```
. . .
spring.mail.host=smtp.gmail.com
spring.mail.port=587
spring.mail.username=username
spring.mail.password=password
spring.mail.properties.mail.smtp.auth=true
spring.mail.properties.mail.smtp.starttls.enable=true
```

Here, you will put your real Gmail address, as well as your username and password, instead of the ones we gave in the example!

Now create the implementation for `NotesCountNotificationService`. Give the class the name `NotesCountNotificationServiceImpl` and the following implementation:

```
package com.journaler.api.reactor

import com.journaler.api.mail.MailMessage
import com.journaler.api.mail.MailService
import org.springframework.beans.factory.annotation.Autowired
import org.springframework.stereotype.Service

@Service
class NotesCountNotificationServiceImpl : NotesCountNotificationService {

    @Autowired
    private lateinit var mailService: MailService

    override fun notify(notification: NotesCountNotification) {
        val to = "go.reactive.with.spring@mailinator.com"
        val subject = "Notes count notification"
        val text = "Notes reached ${notification.notesCount} count."
        val message = MailMessage(to, subject, text)
        mailService.sendMessage(message)
    }

}
```

We also need the implementation for `TodosCountNotificationService`:

```
package com.journaler.api.reactor

import com.journaler.api.mail.MailMessage
import com.journaler.api.mail.MailService
import org.springframework.beans.factory.annotation.Autowired
import org.springframework.stereotype.Service

@Service
class TodosCountNotificationServiceImpl : TodosCountNotificationService {

    @Autowired
    private lateinit var mailService: MailService

    override fun notify(notification: TodosCountNotification) {
        val to = "go.reactive.with.spring@mailinator.com"
        val subject = "Notes count notification"
        val text = "Todos reached ${notification.todosCount} count."
        val message = MailMessage(to, subject, text)
        mailService.sendMessage(message)
```

```
        }

    }
```

The implementation does the same thing as it does for the `Note` entity by sending an email message about entity count in the system. For both implementations, replace the `to` value of `go.reactive.with.spring@mailinator.com` with your desired destination email address.

To be able to map notifications to the Project React event bus, we must define the consumer class. Create a new interface inside the reactor package called `NotificationConsumer`:

```
package com.journaler.api.reactor

import reactor.bus.Event
import reactor.fn.Consumer

interface NotificationConsumer<T> : Consumer<Event<T>>
```

We will have two implementations. The first one will be `NotesCountNotificationConsumer`:

```
package com.journaler.api.reactor

import org.springframework.beans.factory.annotation.Autowired
import org.springframework.stereotype.Service
import reactor.bus.Event

@Service
class NotesCountNotificationConsumer :
NotificationConsumer<NotesCountNotification> {

    @Autowired
    lateinit var service: NotesCountNotificationService

    override fun accept(e: Event<NotesCountNotification>?) {
        val data = e?.data
        data?.let {
            service.notify(data)
        }
    }

}
```

And the second one will be as follows:

```
package com.journaler.api.reactor

import org.springframework.beans.factory.annotation.Autowired
import org.springframework.stereotype.Service
import reactor.bus.Event

@Service
class TodosCountNotificationConsumer :
NotificationConsumer<TodosCountNotification> {

    @Autowired
    lateinit var service: TodosCountNotificationService

    override fun accept(e: Event<TodosCountNotification>?) {
        val data = e?.data
        data?.let {
            service.notify(data)
        }
    }

}
```

Finally, we will change our code so that we are able to transmit events. Open `NoteService` and update its implementation:

```
package com.journaler.api.service

import com.journaler.api.data.Note
import com.journaler.api.data.NoteDTO
import com.journaler.api.reactor.NotesCountNotification
import com.journaler.api.repository.NoteRepository
import org.springframework.beans.factory.annotation.Autowired
import org.springframework.stereotype.Service
import reactor.bus.Event
import reactor.bus.EventBus
import java.util.*

@Service
class NoteService {
    ...
    @Autowired
    private lateinit var eventBus: EventBus
    ...
    fun insertNote(note: NoteDTO): NoteDTO {
        val result = NoteDTO(
```

```
                repository.save(
                        Note(
                                title = note.title,
                                message = note.message,
                                location = note.location
                        )
                )
        )
        val count = getNotes().count()
        if (count > 10) {
            val notification = NotesCountNotification(count)
            eventBus.notify("notesCountNotificationConsumer",
Event.wrap(notification))
        }
        return result
    }
    ...
}
```

And do the same change for the `TodoService` class:

```
package com.journaler.api.service

import com.journaler.api.data.Todo
import com.journaler.api.data.TodoDTO
import com.journaler.api.reactor.TodosCountNotification
import com.journaler.api.repository.TodoRepository
import org.springframework.beans.factory.annotation.Autowired
import org.springframework.stereotype.Service
import reactor.bus.Event
import reactor.bus.EventBus
import java.util.*


@Service
class TodoService {
    ...
    @Autowired
    private lateinit var eventBus: EventBus
    ...
    fun insertTodo(todo: TodoDTO): TodoDTO {
        val result = TodoDTO(
                repository.save(
                        Todo(
                                title = todo.title,
                                message = todo.message,
                                location = todo.location,
                                schedule = todo.schedule
```

```
                )
            )
        )
        val count = getTodos().count()
        if (count > 10) {
            val notification = TodosCountNotification(count)
            eventBus.notify("todosCountNotificationConsumer",
    Event.wrap(notification))
        }
        return result
    }
    ...
}
```

Every time we insert a new entity, we will check for the count and, if the total count is larger than 10, we will transmit the event. We used the `EventBus` class to send a wrapped notification. Since we still don't have an `EventBus` candidate for injecting, we must provide one. Also, here we will connect all parts together and make our code ready for execution.

Open the `ApiApplication` application class and extend it:

```
package com.journaler.api

import com.journaler.api.reactor.NotesCountNotificationConsumer
import com.journaler.api.reactor.TodosCountNotificationConsumer
import org.springframework.beans.factory.annotation.Autowired
import org.springframework.boot.CommandLineRunner
import org.springframework.boot.SpringApplication
import org.springframework.boot.autoconfigure.SpringBootApplication
import org.springframework.cloud.netflix.eureka.EnableEurekaClient
import org.springframework.context.annotation.Bean
import reactor.Environment
import reactor.bus.EventBus
import reactor.bus.selector.Selectors.`$`


@SpringBootApplication
@EnableEurekaClient
class ApiApplication : CommandLineRunner {

    @Autowired
    private lateinit var eventBus: EventBus

    @Autowired
    private lateinit var notesCountNotificationConsumer:
NotesCountNotificationConsumer
```

```
    @Autowired
    private lateinit var todosCountNotificationConsumer:
TodosCountNotificationConsumer

    @Bean
    fun env() = Environment.initializeIfEmpty().assignErrorJournal()

    @Bean
    fun createEventBus(env: Environment) = EventBus.create(env,
Environment.THREAD_POOL)

    override fun run(vararg args: String) {
        eventBus.on(`$`("notesCountNotificationConsumer"),
notesCountNotificationConsumer)
        eventBus.on(`$`("todosCountNotificationConsumer"),
todosCountNotificationConsumer)
    }
}

fun main(args: Array<String>) {
    SpringApplication.run(ApiApplication::class.java, *args)
}
```

What did we just do? First of all, we extended CommandLineRunner with the following code:

```
package org.springframework.boot;

import org.springframework.core.Ordered;
import org.springframework.core.annotation.Order;

public interface CommandLineRunner {

    /**
     * Callback used to run the bean.
     * @param args incoming main method arguments
     * @throws Exception on error
     */
    void run(String... args) throws Exception;

}
```

The preceding interface is used to indicate that a bean should run when it's contained within the Spring application. Multiple CommandLineRunner beans can be defined within the same application context and can be ordered using the Ordered interface or @Ordered annotation.

With the following code block, we initialize `EventBus`:

```
@Autowired
private lateinit var eventBus: EventBus

@Autowired
private lateinit var notesCountNotificationConsumer:
NotesCountNotificationConsumer

@Autowired
private lateinit var todosCountNotificationConsumer:
TodosCountNotificationConsumer

@Bean
fun env() = Environment.initializeIfEmpty().assignErrorJournal()

@Bean
fun createEventBus(env: Environment) = EventBus.create(env,
Environment.THREAD_POOL)

override fun run(vararg args: String) {
    eventBus.on(`$`("notesCountNotificationConsumer"),
notesCountNotificationConsumer)
    eventBus.on(`$`("todosCountNotificationConsumer"),
todosCountNotificationConsumer)
}
```

Here, EventBus is initialized with the default thread pool from the environment. We also mapped our consumers and now we are ready to try our REST API. Start your local Redis server and run all services one by one: configuration, discovery, gateway, and finally the Journaler API. Log in to the Gmail account you defined in your configuration from the web browser. Open Postman and insert a couple of notes and TODOs. After you reach a count of more than 10 items, you should get an email message.

 It may be the case that you have problems using Gmail SMTP servers or you don't have access to an SMTP server at all. In that case, you need to update your implementation to just log notifications instead of trying to send email messages.

Open `NotesCountNotificationServiceImpl` and update it:

```
package com.journaler.api.reactor

import org.springframework.stereotype.Service

@Service
class NotesCountNotificationServiceImpl : NotesCountNotificationService {

    override fun notify(notification: NotesCountNotification) {
        val text = "Notes reached ${notification.notesCount} count."
        println("NOTIFICATION >>>>> $text")
    }

}
```

Do the same with `TodosCountNotificationServiceImpl`:

```
package com.journaler.api.reactor

import org.springframework.stereotype.Service

@Service
class TodosCountNotificationServiceImpl : TodosCountNotificationService {

    override fun notify(notification: TodosCountNotification) {
        val text = "Todos reached ${notification.todosCount} count."
        println("NOTIFICATION >>>>> $text")
    }

}
```

Rerun all services again and retry. You will notice log output similar to the following:

Summary

Making things reactive is a frequent requirement for many modern applications. In this chapter, we demonstrated how to make this functionality available to your services easily and quickly. Think about the possible benefit of using an event bus and try to extend existing API service applications to support more events. Finally, prepare yourself for a discussion about Spring practices, since that will be our focus in the next chapter.

8
Development Practices

In everyday development, you will come into contact with different practices. Some of them might not be so good because they are unsafe or costly in terms of performance. Developers frequently argue about the efficacy of these practices. In this chapter, we will focus on some of the most common and important practices and challenge them.

In this chapter, we will learn about the following:

- Different development practices
- Some bad development practices
- Some good development practices

Challenging development practices

We can say that Spring Framework development is straightforward and that there are few chances to make mistakes. That is mostly true. However, we will challenge some of the most commonly used Spring Framework features and discuss some of their drawbacks.

Reviewing dependency injection

As you already know, `@Autowired` is the magic word that makes our lives easier. We inject the proper instance for the field and make it available in our code. Field injection is easy to do and very popular. The code we have is clear and easy to read and maintain. But there is something you should know about it!

Let's consider injecting our dependencies through the constructor. If we have one dependency, we will inject constructor that have for example one parameter. As the number of dependencies rises, the number of constructor parameters rises, too. Fortunately, this isn't a problem in Kotlin, where we have single-line constructors. At some point, you will realize that by injecting so many dependencies, you assigned too many responsibilities to your class and that further refactoring is required. By using `@Autowired`, you won't have this problem! So, be careful and pay attention to the number of injected fields.

By increasing the complexity of the project, the number of required dependencies rises, as well. Soon, it could be very difficult to distinguish how everything is bound together.

Making your classes too open

Many developers tend to have too many exposed classes, that is, have an overly publicly visible code. Making the internal structure too open decreases the flexibility of your code and increases the risk of issues. An example of this could be skipping a whole layer and directly accessing class methods and properties that shouldn't be accessed directly.

Mutability

Leaving your variables mutable is not always a good idea. For example, a variable can be modified even before you gain access to it. Wherever possible, you should configure your variables so they can be constants or can't be changed anymore once they get their value (having getter exposed only).

Multithreading

As with any other software, multithreading can be an issue. Developers frequently tend to do it wrong. Debugging problematic multithreading applications can be an issue, too. So, what are the problems with multithreading practices? Here are a few:

- The first cause of a headache can come from globally visible and modifiable variables. Leaving your variables global opens doors for a lot of issues. Debugging issues that come from this can become a nightmare.
- The second cause can be the spawning of too many threads. If you do so, this can affect the performance of your application significantly. We will suggest proper practice for this in the next sections.

- Also, developers tend not to name their threads. Assign meaningful names to your threads so debugging and tracking can be easier!

Not validating data

One of the common causes of issues in your software is not validating the data you deal with. Sometimes we don't validate the length of expected fields, email addresses, and other data. Passing invalid data to components of our system is the source of malfunctions or even crashes.

Tests coverage

Another bad practice is not writing unit tests. The worst scenario is not having any at all! Not covering all your classes with tests isn't much better. Why is this important? This is important not just because tests prove that all components behave properly, but they also serve as documentation for our code. We will talk more about unit testing in the next chapter, where we will give you guidance on how to write them.

XML configurations

XML configurations were what we used to configure Spring applications. Configuring Spring applications through XML was the source of a lot of boilerplate code. Luckily for us, Spring 5 applications do not require this way of configuring. We use proper annotations instead, as we did in all examples in this book.

Good ways to develop your code

Since we just challenged some of Spring Framework's most important features and practices, now it's time to shed some light on good ways of developing your code. Let's start again with dependency injection.

Don't inject too much

As we already mentioned, the @Autowired annotation will inject all necessary dependencies. To avoid the problem with dependency injection that we explained previously, try to avoid injecting too many dependencies into a single class. Usually, it's good if you have very few beans that your class requires. It's up to you to maintain this balance and organize your architecture.

Use a closed-visibility approach

To avoid problems caused by exposing your methods and fields publicly, consider making them at least package-level visible at first. Ideally, all fields encapsulated in your classes should be private or protected, or at package-level visibility. Expose those fields or methods only if needed. Consider the consequences of giving access to the functionalities of methods to the outside world.

Solving the multithreading issue

There is no single solution for solving problems with the multithreading practices that we described previously. All solutions are dependent on the nature of the specific problem you have, as well as the existing architecture of your software.

For example, the solution to the problem of having your variables globally visible and modifiable can be prevented by using synchronization—but that can be costly in terms of performance. So, once again, think twice if you intend to expose something globally. There can be other ways to achieve the same goal.

If you have a tendency to create a lot of new threads running for the same functionalities, a better solution could be to have only one thread running and performing the same operation when needed. If we constantly start a new thread for the same operations and we do that frequently, our performance and memory will be wasted on garbage collection, for example.

When dealing with threads, we also recommend using proper classes instead of triggering naked threads directly. Use ExecutorService abstractions so there is more control over thread execution. By doing this, you can limit the maximal number of threads running at the same time or the maximal number of threads to be put in a queue.

Spring data validation

Let's face the problem we discussed earlier: not validating data. Spring Framework provides us with a set of validators, thanks to which we can validate any kind of data we deal with. Also, it is possible to write your custom validators if needed by implementing the following interface:

```
org.springframework.validation.Validator
```

We will take a look at the most commonly used validators:

- `@Length`: To validate a variable for length
- `@Email`: To validate an email address
- `@NonNull`: To validate not being null
- `@Null`: To validate being null
- `@NotBlank`: To validate that the annotated string is not null or empty; the difference here to `@NotEmpty` being that trailing whitespaces are ignored
- `@NotEmpty`: To validate that the annotated string is not null or empty
- `@Range`: To validate that an annotated element is in the appropriate range
- `@SafeHtml`: To validate a rich-text value provided by the user to ensure that it contains no malicious code
- `@URL`: To validate a URL

If the previously mentioned validators do not satisfy your needs, you can always write your own validator implementation. Let's give a quick example of a custom validator:

```
package com.journaler.api.validator

import com.journaler.api.data.NoteDTO
import org.springframework.stereotype.Component
import org.springframework.validation.Errors
import org.springframework.validation.Validator

@Component
class NoteValidator : Validator {

    override fun validate(target: Any?, errors: Errors?) {
        if (target is NoteDTO) {
            when (target) {
                // Reject if example pattern 'x x x x' occurs.
                target.title.contains("x x x x") ->
errors?.rejectValue("title", "Not allowed!")
            }
```

```
            return
        }
        errors?.rejectValue("title", "Only String titles allowed")
    }

    override fun supports(clazz: Class<*>?): Boolean {
        return NoteDTO::class.java == clazz
    }
}
```

As you can see, all you have to do is implement an interface and apply the validation in the validate method implementation.

Summary

Discussion of good software and development practices in Spring is an endless topic. In this chapter, we identified some of the most important practices to consider. Try to think about the good and bad practices we discussed and, most importantly, try to practice them for a while. You will notice that the quality of the applications you develop will improve significantly. Also, try to be open-minded regarding other good practice suggestions and think about how you could benefit from them. Most importantly, avoid bad practices since many of them can lead you astray.

In the next chapter, we will cover one particularly good development practice: we will write unit tests for our code. We will demonstrate how to write tests and provide guidance on how to make use of them. Be patient, try every example that follows, and consider how you could use them to test some of your own components.

9
Testing

To be able to develop good software, writing tests is mandatory. Writing tests will prove that your code is working properly and help you detect issues the QA teams would not find otherwise. In this chapter, we will guide you through testing guidelines and show you practical examples of how to do it. We will start by explaining the importance of testing and then continue towards practical steps in tests, including writing and common testing practices.

In this chapter, we will talk about the following:

- Why is testing a crucial part of development?
- Some bad development practices
- Some good development practices

Why is testing a crucial part of development?

Automated testing is a great way to check if the code you wrote is working. Tests check whether our software is working properly and will keep on working the way we intend it to. There are many different approaches and practices of writing tests. In this chapter, we will mention some of them.

Before the QA team starts testing the product, developers should make sure that all classes are covered with proper tests and that all of the tests are passing. When the development team does not care about writing proper tests or does not cover most (ideally all) of the codebase with tests, the QA team will most likely experience problems in testing and raise issues.

So, what are the benefits of testing? First of all, code which has been covered by tests has fewer bugs. Also, it makes it easier to keep track of documentation, and improves software design in general.

By utilizing testing code, it's easier to reuse. You can easily reuse your tests and the codebase in new projects. Writing tests will improve your understanding of the code you are working on.

Some major benefits of tests are improving classes including visibility, decoupling, and better organization, and this will make your code easier to maintain and extend. Writing tests for your codebase that is already covered with tests will be a routine.

If we write our tests during the development phase, we will be able to catch bugs in the early stages of development so that, in the final phases, we will have minimal or no bugs at all. Thanks to testing, we will achieve the following benefits:

- Better visibility
- Better error reporting
- Development efficiency
- Speed
- Practicability of system behavior
- Easier planning

So, what is testing?

To summarize, testing represents the kind of testing where a developer usually writes tests that are performed on the source code of the project. All testing that is performed is done by knowing everything about the source code that is being tested. In ideal scenarios, a person who writes tests would perform testing on each class of the source code. Thanks to this, we can be sure that all of our code is behaving as we expect it to.

Common test practices and approaches

Let's start by noting some points that all tests must fulfill:

- Every team member must be able to run tests or test collections we created with no significant effort
- **Continuous integration** (**CI**) servers must be able to run these tests out of the box without any need for additional actions

- Results of testing must be unambiguous
- Each time we repeat the tests, we must get the same results

We are going to distinguish several ways of writing tests. One of the ways of writing tests is through **test-driven development** (**TDD**). In TDD, tests are written before your features' implementation code. Tests do assertions for functionalities that your features must fulfill, and then we can start developing those features. Assertions will fail before the implementation is done. As we progress with the implementation, each test will pass until we have covered everything. This approach is typically used when we want to identify requirements of the system and to allow regression testing of all of our features, especially if some changes are done.

Some developers tend to write tests after the features are implemented. Usually, when this is the case, it is necessary to use some code coverage tools so that they identify the percentage of code covered with tests.

Preparing our project

Before we start writing tests, we will make some changes in our `build.gradle` configuration:

```
buildscript {
    ext {
        kotlinVersion = '1.2.21'
        springBootVersion = '2.0.0.M4'
    }
    repositories {
        mavenCentral()
        maven { url "https://repo.spring.io/snapshot" }
        maven { url "https://repo.spring.io/milestone" }
    }
    dependencies {
        classpath("org.springframework.boot:spring-boot-gradle-
plugin:${springBootVersion}")
        classpath("org.jetbrains.kotlin:kotlin-gradle-
plugin:${kotlinVersion}")
        classpath("org.jetbrains.kotlin:kotlin-allopen:${kotlinVersion}")
    }
}

apply plugin: 'kotlin'
apply plugin: 'kotlin-spring'
apply plugin: 'eclipse'
```

```
apply plugin: 'org.springframework.boot'
apply plugin: 'io.spring.dependency-management'

group = 'com.journaler'
version = '0.0.1-SNAPSHOT'
sourceCompatibility = 1.8

compileKotlin {
    kotlinOptions.jvmTarget = "1.8"
}
compileTestKotlin {
    kotlinOptions.jvmTarget = "1.8"
}

repositories {
    mavenCentral()
    maven { url "https://repo.spring.io/snapshot" }
    maven { url "https://repo.spring.io/milestone" }
}

dependencies {
    compile 'org.springframework.boot:spring-boot-starter-security'
    compile 'org.springframework:spring-context'
    compile 'org.springframework:spring-aop'
    compile 'org.springframework.boot:spring-boot-starter'
    compile 'org.springframework.boot:spring-boot-starter-web'
    compile 'org.springframework.boot:spring-boot-starter-actuator'
    compile 'org.springframework:spring-web'
    compile 'org.springframework:spring-webmvc'
    runtime 'mysql:mysql-connector-java'
    compile 'org.springframework.boot:spring-boot-starter-data-jpa'
    compile "org.jetbrains.kotlin:kotlin-stdlib-jdk8:${kotlinVersion}"
    compile "org.jetbrains.kotlin:kotlin-reflect:${kotlinVersion}"
    testCompile 'org.springframework.boot:spring-boot-starter-test'
}
```

We updated our dependencies to match the version of Kotlin that is included with IntelliJ IDE. Take a look if you have a warning message regarding that, and make sure that your `build.gradle` configuration follows the version your IntelliJ IDE has. To be sure about what exactly we are changing, take a look at this diff:

The difference between the previous and the current build.gradle configuration

We will simplify our application a bit so it's easier to demonstrate the test writing procedure. We will remove Reactor and apply some changes. Remove the following files:

- `bootsrtap.properties` (we don't want complex configuration at the moment)
- `MailMessage.kt`
- `MailService.kt`
- `MailServiceImpl.kt`
- `NotesCountNotification.kt`
- `NotesCountNotificationConsumer.kt`
- `NotesCountNotificationService.kt`
- `NotesCountNotificationServiceImpl.kt`
- `NotificationConsumer.kt`
- `NotificationService.kt`
- `SessionConfiguration.kt`
- `TodosCountNotification.kt`
- `TodosCountNotificationConsumer.kt`
- `TodosCountNotificationService.kt`
- `TodosCountNotificationServiceImpl.kt`

Then, create the `application.properties` file again:

```
spring.application.name= journaler
server.port= 9000
logging.level.root=INFO
logging.level.com.journaler.api=DEBUG
logging.level.org.springframework.jdbc=ERROR

endpoints.health.enabled=true
endpoints.trace.enabled=true
endpoints.info.enabled=true
endpoints.metrics.enabled=true

spring.datasource.url=jdbc:mysql://localhost/journaler_api?useSSL=false&use
Unicode=true&characterEncoding=utf-8
spring.datasource.username=root
spring.datasource.password=localInstance2017
spring.datasource.tomcat.test-on-borrow=true
spring.datasource.tomcat.validation-interval=30000
spring.datasource.tomcat.validation-query=SELECT 1
spring.datasource.tomcat.remove-abandoned=true
spring.datasource.tomcat.remove-abandoned-timeout=10000
spring.datasource.tomcat.log-abandoned=true
spring.datasource.tomcat.max-age=1800000
spring.datasource.tomcat.log-validation-errors=true
spring.datasource.tomcat.max-active=50
spring.datasource.tomcat.max-idle=10

spring.jpa.hibernate.ddl-auto=update
```

Update the `ApiApplication` class like so:

```
package com.journaler.api

import org.springframework.boot.SpringApplication
import org.springframework.boot.autoconfigure.SpringBootApplication

@SpringBootApplication
class ApiApplication

fun main(args: Array<String>) {
    SpringApplication.run(ApiApplication::class.java, *args)
}
```

And update the services accordingly:

- NoteService:

```
package com.journaler.api.service

import com.journaler.api.data.Note
import com.journaler.api.data.NoteDTO
import com.journaler.api.repository.NoteRepository
import org.springframework.beans.factory.annotation.Autowired
import org.springframework.stereotype.Service
import java.util.*

@Service("Note service")
class NoteService {

    @Autowired
    lateinit var repository: NoteRepository

    fun getNotes(): Iterable<NoteDTO> = repository.findAll().map {
it -> NoteDTO(it) }

    fun insertNote(note: NoteDTO) = NoteDTO(
            repository.save(
                    Note(
                            title = note.title,
                            message = note.message,
                            location = note.location
                    )
            )
    )

    fun deleteNote(id: String) = repository.deleteById(id)

    fun updateNote(noteDto: NoteDTO): NoteDTO {
        val note = repository.findById(noteDto.id).get()
        note.title = noteDto.title
        note.message = noteDto.message
        note.location = noteDto.location
        note.modified = Date()
        return NoteDTO(repository.save(note))
    }

    fun findByTitle(title: String): Iterable<NoteDTO> {
        return repository.findByTitle(title).map { it ->
NoteDTO(it) }
```

```
                }

        }

    • TodoService:

        package com.journaler.api.service

        import com.journaler.api.data.Todo
        import com.journaler.api.data.TodoDTO
        import com.journaler.api.repository.TodoRepository
        import org.springframework.beans.factory.annotation.Autowired
        import org.springframework.stereotype.Service
        import java.util.*


        @Service("Todo service")
        class TodoService {

            @Autowired
            lateinit var repository: TodoRepository

            fun getTodos(): Iterable<TodoDTO> = repository.findAll().map {
        it -> TodoDTO(it) }

            fun insertTodo(todo: TodoDTO) = TodoDTO(
                    repository.save(
                            Todo(
                                    title = todo.title,
                                    message = todo.message,
                                    location = todo.location,
                                    schedule = todo.schedule


                            )
                    )
            )

            fun deleteTodo(id: String) = repository.deleteById(id)

            fun updateTodo(todoDto: TodoDTO): TodoDTO {
                val todo = repository.findById(todoDto.id).get()
                todo.title = todoDto.title
                todo.message = todoDto.message
                todo.location = todoDto.location
                todo.schedule = todoDto.schedule
                todo.modified = Date()
                return TodoDTO(repository.save(todo))
            }
```

```
fun getScheduledLaterThan(date: Date?): Iterable<TodoDTO> {
    date?.let {
        return repository.findScheduledLaterThan(date.time).map
{ it -> TodoDTO(it) }
    }
    return listOf()
}

}
```

Writing our first test with Kotlin

In this section, we will start with a slow introduction to test writing by creating a couple of simple tests. Locate your src/test directory and, under the com.journaler package, create a new class called NoteTest:

```
package com.journaler

import org.junit.Test

class NoteTest {

    @Test
    fun testNoteInsert(){
    }

}
```

We just defined an empty test that, at this point, doesn't do anything. Despite this, we introduced some very important things. We used the @Test annotation that will tell the test framework which method will represent test implementation. We are not limited to only one test per test class, so let's add a couple more tests in our test class:

```
package com.journaler

import org.junit.Test

class NoteTest {
    @Test
    fun testNoteInsert(){
    }

    @Test
    fun testNoteUpdate(){
    }
```

```
    @Test
    fun testNoteDelete(){
    }

    @Test
    fun testNoteSelect(){
    }
}
```

Now, we have four tests in our `NoteTest` class with no actual implementation. As we are aware that each method will actually test something, we don't need this `prefix` in the name of each method:

```
package com.journaler

import org.junit.Test

class NoteTest {
    @Test
    fun noteInsert(){
    }

    @Test
    fun noteUpdate(){
    }

    @Test
    fun noteDelete(){
    }

    @Test
    fun noteSelect(){
    }
}
```

Actually, we don't need the `note` prefix either since the `NoteTest` class will be dedicated to only testing the `Note` entity:

```
package com.journaler

import org.junit.Test

class NoteTest {
    @Test
    fun insert(){
    }
```

```
    @Test
    fun update(){
    }

    @Test
    fun delete(){
    }

    @Test
    fun select(){
    }
}
```

Now, let's say we have some requirements for preparing the environment to run these four tests, and an additional cleanup after each of our tests has been completed. We need to introduce two new annotations:

```
package com.journaler

import org.junit.After
import org.junit.Before
import org.junit.Test

class NoteTest {
    @Before
    fun prepare(){
        // Prepare environment and requirements for tests to be performed.
    }

    @Test
    fun insert(){
        // Test insert operation for Note entity.
    }

    @Test
    fun update(){
        // Test update operation for Note entity.
    }

    @Test
    fun delete(){
        // Test delete operation for Note entity.
    }

    @Test
    fun select(){
        // Test select operation for Note entity.
```

```
        }

    @After
    fun cleanup(){
        // Do cleanup after all tests are performed.
    }
}
```

As you can see, we introduced the `@Before` and `@After` annotations. These mark the methods that will be performed before and after these four tests. This means that when each test is performed, we will trigger the `prepare()` and `cleanup()` methods. Tests method invocation ordering is not guaranteed! So, what will happen if we run the tests a couple of times? To get an answer to this question, we need to put some output in our tests:

```
package com.journaler

import org.junit.After
import org.junit.Before
import org.junit.Test

class NoteTest {
    @Before
    fun prepare() {
        println("Prepare.")
        // Prepare environment and requirements for tests to be performed.
    }

    @Test
    fun insert() {
        println("Insert.")
        // Test insert operation for Note entity.
    }

    @Test
    fun update() {
        println("Update.")
        // Test update operation for Note entity.
    }

    @Test
    fun delete() {
        println("Delete.")
        // Test delete operation for Note entity.
    }

    @Test
    fun select() {
```

```
    println("Select.")
    // Test select operation for Note entity.
}

@After
fun cleanup() {
    println("Cleanup.")
    // Do cleanup after all tests are performed.
}
}
```

Run the test three times. Let's see what output we get:

- With iteration 1, we get the following:
  - Prepare
  - Delete
  - Cleanup
  - Prepare
  - Insert
  - Cleanup
  - Prepare
  - Select
  - Cleanup
  - Prepare
  - Update
  - Cleanup

- With iteration 2, we get the following:
  - Prepare
  - Delete
  - Cleanup
  - Prepare
  - Insert
  - Cleanup
  - Prepare
  - Select
  - Cleanup
  - Prepare

- Update
- Cleanup

- With iteration 3, we get the following:
  - Prepare
  - Delete
  - Cleanup
  - Prepare
  - Insert
  - Cleanup
  - Prepare
  - Select
  - Cleanup
  - Prepare
  - Update
  - Cleanup

As you can see, each time the order was the same, but not in the order we defined the tests in the `NoteTest` class. Let's do something about this. Update your `NoteTest` class implementation like this:

```kotlin
package com.journaler

import org.junit.After
import org.junit.Before
import org.junit.Test

class NoteTest {
    @Before
    fun prepare() {
        println("Prepare.")
        // Prepare environment and requirements for tests to be performed.
    }

    @Test
    fun crud() {
        // Test Note entity CRUD operations.
        insert()
        update()
        delete()
        select()
```

```
    }

    @After
    fun cleanup() {
        println("Cleanup.")
        // Do cleanup after all tests are performed.
    }

    fun insert() {
        println("Insert.")
        // Test insert operation for Note entity.
    }

    fun update() {
        println("Update.")
        // Test update operation for Note entity.
    }

    fun delete() {
        println("Delete.")
        // Test delete operation for Note entity.
    }

    fun select() {
        println("Select.")
        // Test select operation for Note entity.
    }
}
```

Now, we have one test that will trigger the test steps in the order we require. Running this test will give us the following output:

- `Prepare`
- `Insert`
- `Update`
- `Delete`
- `Select`
- `Cleanup`

Note that now we have the `prepare()` and `cleanup()` methods invoked only once.

Running the test in InteliJ IDEA

Let's run this test in IntelliJ IDEA. Follow these steps:

1. Locate the test file in the hierarchy as shown in the following screenshot:

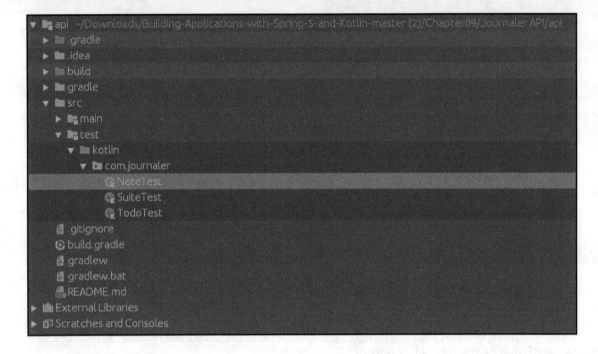

2. Right-click on it and choose **Run 'NoteTest'**, as shown in the following screenshot:

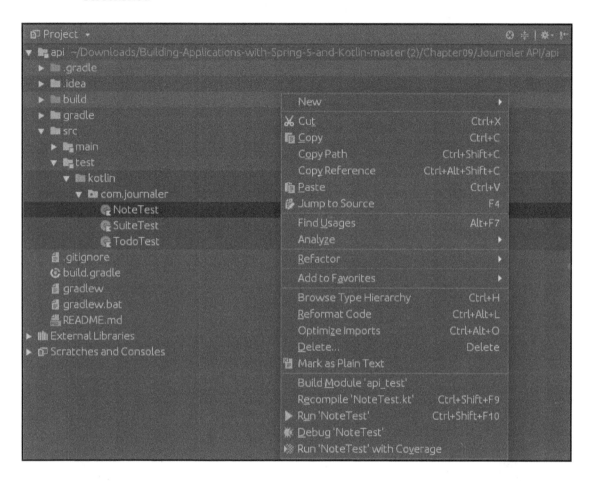

3. The test will be executed. Wait while it finishes and observes the test results, as shown in the following screenshot:

4. IntelliJ IDEA automatically creates the configuration for you. So, if you expand the available configuration at the top of the window, you will see **NoteTest** configuration, as shown in the following screenshot:

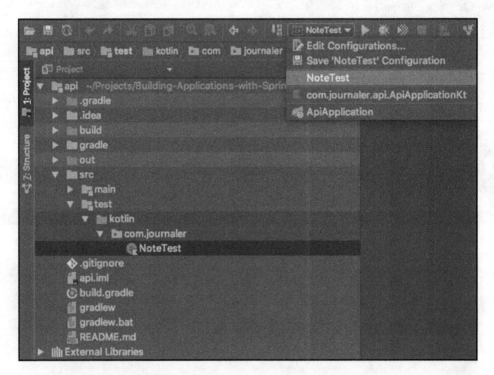

5. Click on it to choose the configuration and then click on the **Run** button to run the test once more.

Testing Spring REST applications

In this section, we will continue towards test implementation and will be testing Spring-specific topics. First of all, we will specify the `SprintRunner` class, which is going to be used as the test runner for our tests:

```
package com.journaler

import org.junit.After
import org.junit.Before
import org.junit.Test
import org.junit.runner.RunWith
import org.springframework.test.context.junit4.SpringRunner

@RunWith(SpringRunner::class)
class NoteTest {
    ...
}
```

By annotating `@RunWith(SpringRunner::class)`, we specified that `SpringRunner` will be used for test running and will be initializing `TestContextManager` to provide Spring testing functionality to standard tests. Let's run the test once more. Observe the output in the following screenshot:

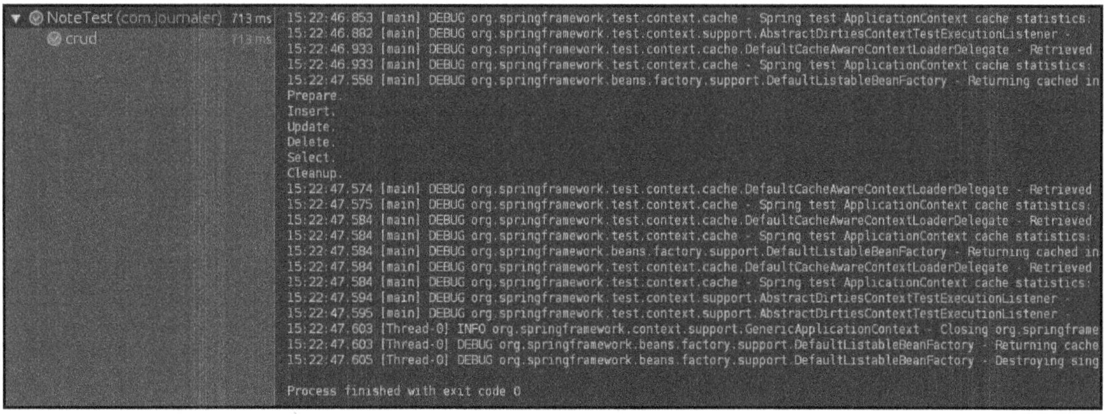

As you can see, Spring Framework is being used to support the test we just run.

As we already know, the `NoteTest` class doesn't have any implementation. We will test the Service layer of our application, and we will add some code so that the test can actually check something. We will inject `NoteService` and assert that it is instantiated:

```
package com.journaler

import com.journaler.api.ApiApplication
import com.journaler.api.data.NoteDTO
import com.journaler.api.service.NoteService
import org.junit.After
import org.junit.Assert
import org.junit.Before
import org.junit.Test
import org.junit.runner.RunWith
import org.springframework.beans.factory.annotation.Autowired
import org.springframework.boot.test.context.SpringBootTest
import org.springframework.test.context.junit4.SpringRunner

@RunWith(SpringRunner::class)
@SpringBootTest(classes = [ApiApplication::class])
class NoteTest {

    @Autowired
    private lateinit var service: NoteService

    @Before
    fun prepare() {
        println("Prepare.")
        Assert.assertNotNull(service)
    }

    @Test
    fun crud() {
        // Test Note entity CRUD operations.
        insert()
        update()
        delete()
        select()
    }

    @After
    fun cleanup() {
        println("Cleanup.")
        // Do cleanup after all tests are performed.
    }
```

```
fun insert() {
    println("Insert.")
}

fun update() {
    println("Update.")
    // Test update operation for Note entity.
}

fun delete() {
    println("Delete.")
}

fun select() {
    println("Select.")
    // Test select operation for Note entity.
}
}
```

We successfully injected the `NoteService` class and asserted it. We also introduced one very important annotation: `@SpringBootTest`. This annotation can be specified on test classes that run Spring Boot-based tests. It provides the following features over the regular Spring TestContext Framework, as the class documentation specifies:

- Uses `SpringBootContextLoader` as the default `ContextLoader` when no specific `@ContextConfiguration(loader=...)` is defined
- Automatically searches for a `@SpringBootConfiguration` when the nested `@Configuration` is not used, and no explicit classes are specified
- Allows custom environment properties to be defined using the properties attribute
- Provides support for different web environment modes, including the ability to start a fully running container listening on a defined or random port
- Registers a `TestRestTemplate` bean for use in web tests that are using a fully running container

Run your test; it must pass, as shown in the following screenshot:

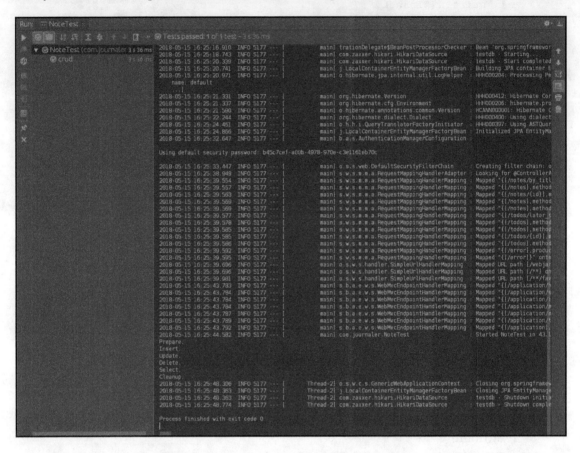

We now have everything we need in order to test the service layer for notes. Let's write some test implementation to verify the service layer's functionality:

```
package com.journaler

import com.journaler.api.ApiApplication
import com.journaler.api.data.NoteDTO
import com.journaler.api.service.NoteService
import org.junit.After
import org.junit.Assert
import org.junit.Before
import org.junit.Test
import org.junit.runner.RunWith
import org.springframework.beans.factory.annotation.Autowired
import org.springframework.boot.test.context.SpringBootTest
```

```
import org.springframework.test.context.junit4.SpringRunner

@RunWith(SpringRunner::class)
@SpringBootTest(classes = [ApiApplication::class])
class NoteTest {

    @Autowired
    private lateinit var service: NoteService

    private val notes = mutableListOf<NoteDTO>()

    @Before
    fun prepare() {
        Assert.assertNotNull(service)
        // We will prepare 10 Note instances to be inserted:
        (0..10).mapTo(notes) {
            NoteDTO(
                    "Stub note title: $it",
                    "Stub note message: $it"
            )
        }
    }

    @Test
    fun crud() {
        // Test Note entity CRUD operations.
        cleanup()   // We will empty database before run test.
        insert()    // We will insert all prepared Note instances into
database.
        update()    // We will update each Note.
        select()    // We will verify that saved Note instances are valid.
        delete()    // We will remove all Note instances from database.
    }

    fun cleanup() {
        service.getNotes().forEach { note ->
            service.deleteNote(note.id)
        }
    }

    fun insert() {
        notes.forEach { note ->
            val result = service.insertNote(note)
            Assert.assertNotNull(result)
            Assert.assertNotNull(result.id)
            Assert.assertFalse(result.id.isEmpty())
            note.id = result.id
        }
```

```
    }

    fun update() {
        notes.forEach { note ->
            note.title = "updated"
            note.message = "updated"
            val result = service.updateNote(note)
            Assert.assertNotNull(result)
            Assert.assertNotNull(result.id)
            Assert.assertFalse(result.id.isEmpty())
            Assert.assertEquals("updated", result.title)
            Assert.assertEquals("updated", result.message)
        }
    }

    fun delete() {
        notes.forEach { note ->
            println("Removing note with id: ${note.id}")
            service.deleteNote(note.id)
        }
    }

    fun select() {
        val result = service.getNotes()
        result.forEach { note ->
            Assert.assertNotNull(note)
            Assert.assertNotNull(note.id)
            Assert.assertFalse(note.id.isEmpty())
            Assert.assertEquals("updated", note.title)
            Assert.assertEquals("updated", note.message)
        }
    }
}
```

Here, we reorganized the code a bit by using the `cleanup` method to clean up data before the test runs, instead of invoking it after the test. We also switched the order of method execution for the `select()` and `delete()` methods. The implementation of each method should be easy to understand. We are going to perform and verify `crud` operations for the `Note` entity. Then, run your test. It will succeed:

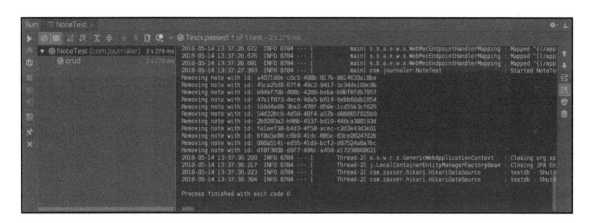

We will write a similar implementation for TODOs. Create the `TodoTest` class and make sure it is implemented like this:

```
package com.journaler

import com.journaler.api.ApiApplication
import com.journaler.api.data.TodoDTO
import com.journaler.api.service.TodoService
import org.junit.Assert
import org.junit.Before
import org.junit.Test
import org.junit.runner.RunWith
import org.springframework.beans.factory.annotation.Autowired
import org.springframework.boot.test.context.SpringBootTest
import org.springframework.test.context.junit4.SpringRunner

@RunWith(SpringRunner::class)
@SpringBootTest(classes = [ApiApplication::class])
class TodoTest {

    @Autowired
    private lateinit var service: TodoService

    private val todos = mutableListOf<TodoDTO>()

    @Before
    fun prepare() {
        Assert.assertNotNull(service)
        // We will prepare 10 instances to be inserted:
        (0..10).mapTo(todos) {
            TodoDTO(
                    "Stub todo title: $it",
```

```
                         "Stub todo message: $it",
                         System.currentTimeMillis()
             )
         }
     }
 }

 @Test
 fun crud() {
     // Test entity CRUD operations.
     cleanup()   // We will empty database before run test.
     insert()    // We will insert all prepared instances into database.
     update()    // We will update each item.
     select()    // We will verify that saved instances are valid.
     delete()    // We will remove all instances from database.
 }

 fun cleanup() {
     service.getTodos().forEach { todo ->
         service.deleteTodo(todo.id)
     }
 }

 fun insert() {
     todos.forEach { todo ->
         val result = service.insertTodo(todo)
         Assert.assertNotNull(result)
         Assert.assertNotNull(result.id)
         Assert.assertFalse(result.id.isEmpty())
         Assert.assertTrue(result.schedule > 0)
         todo.id = result.id
     }
 }

 fun update() {
     todos.forEach { todo ->
         todo.title = "updated"
         todo.message = "updated"
         val result = service.updateTodo(todo)
         Assert.assertNotNull(result)
         Assert.assertNotNull(result.id)
         Assert.assertFalse(result.id.isEmpty())
         Assert.assertEquals("updated", result.title)
         Assert.assertEquals("updated", result.message)
         Assert.assertTrue(result.schedule > 0)
     }
 }

 fun delete() {
```

```
            todos.forEach { todo ->
                println("Removing todo with id: ${todo.id}")
                service.deleteTodo(todo.id)
            }
        }

    fun select() {
        val result = service.getTodos()
        result.forEach { todo ->
            Assert.assertNotNull(todo)
            Assert.assertNotNull(todo.id)
            Assert.assertFalse(todo.id.isEmpty())
            Assert.assertEquals("updated", todo.title)
            Assert.assertEquals("updated", todo.message)
            Assert.assertTrue(todo.schedule > 0)
        }
    }
}
```

We did the same testing as we did for the `Note` entity, except we validated the schedule field that is `TODO` entity specific. You can extend these two tests to verify more attributes if you wish. Run `TodoTest`:

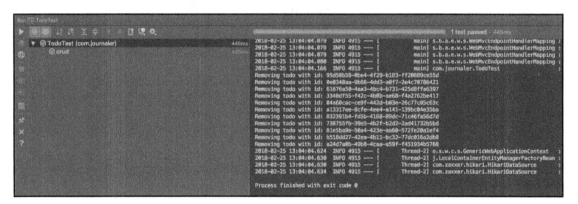

The test will execute successfully.

Running test suites

Imagine you continued writing tests and that you wrote them for a couple more entities. Running them one by one can be frustrating. To make our lives easier, we will create a *container* test which will include all of them. Create a new class called `SuiteTest` and implement it like this:

```
package com.journaler

import org.junit.runner.RunWith
import org.junit.runners.Suite

@RunWith(Suite::class)
@Suite.SuiteClasses(NoteTest::class, TodoTest::class)
class SuiteTest
```

This implementation is easy to understand, but we will highlight the most important parts. The `@Suite.SuiteClasses(NoteTest::class, TodoTest::class)` annotation will define the tests that we will execute. Here comes a list of all of our test classes we want to perform. `@RunWith(Suite::class)` indicates that this test will be executed as a test suite. Now, run the test suite. Observe; we executed both of our tests:

Summary

The exercises we did in this chapter represent just the beginning of a long journey into the world of testing, especially when it comes to testing Spring-specific features. Spring Framework provides us with the tools that are capable of testing each of its components. To better understand Spring Framework testing concepts and capabilities, we recommend that you read the official Spring testing documentation as much as possible or read a book dedicated specifically to this area. For now, it's enough to understand what we presented here, the concept of testing itself, and why it's so important for us. In the next chapter, we will deploy our project and prepare, build, and demonstrate deployment procedures. This is the last piece of the puzzle left!

10
Project Deployment

We have reached the end of our journey. In the previous chapter, we wrote some tests to confirm that our code is working properly. In this chapter, we will release our Spring application into production. We will cover examples of how to publish it step by step and provide you with guidelines and advice for further reading on this subject.

In this final chapter of the book, we will cover the following:

- What will be deployed?
- Deployment options
- Deploying to the Cloud (AWS)

What will be deployed?

Before we deploy anything, we must provide everything that will be deployed. For this, we will deploy the JAR of our API module. The JAR is a result of application building. The first thing we will do is prepare our application for release. We will change our port from 9000 to 80. Open the `application.properties` file and make the following changes:

```
spring.application.name= journaler
server.port= 80
logging.level.root=INFO
logging.level.com.journaler.api=DEBUG
logging.level.org.springframework.jdbc=ERROR

endpoints.health.enabled=true
endpoints.trace.enabled=true
endpoints.info.enabled=true
endpoints.metrics.enabled=true

spring.datasource.url=jdbc:mysql://localhost/journaler_api?useSSL=false&use
Unicode=true&characterEncoding=utf-8
spring.datasource.username=root
```

```
spring.datasource.password=localInstance2017
spring.datasource.tomcat.test-on-borrow=true
spring.datasource.tomcat.validation-interval=30000
spring.datasource.tomcat.validation-query=SELECT 1
spring.datasource.tomcat.remove-abandoned=true
spring.datasource.tomcat.remove-abandoned-timeout=10000
spring.datasource.tomcat.log-abandoned=true
spring.datasource.tomcat.max-age=1800000
spring.datasource.tomcat.log-validation-errors=true
spring.datasource.tomcat.max-active=50
spring.datasource.tomcat.max-idle=10

spring.jpa.hibernate.ddl-auto=update
```

The next thing we need to do is clean the project by executing the `./gradlew clean` command as shown in the following screenshot:

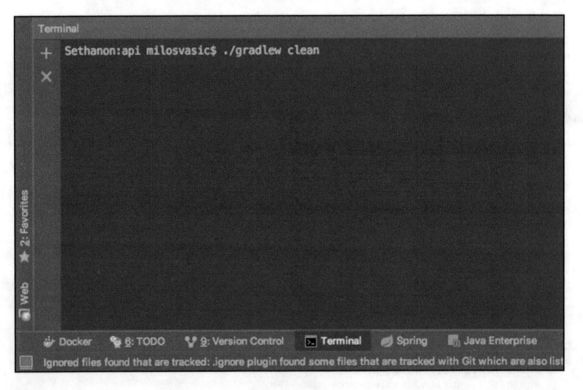

The output of the preceding command is as shown in the following screenshot:

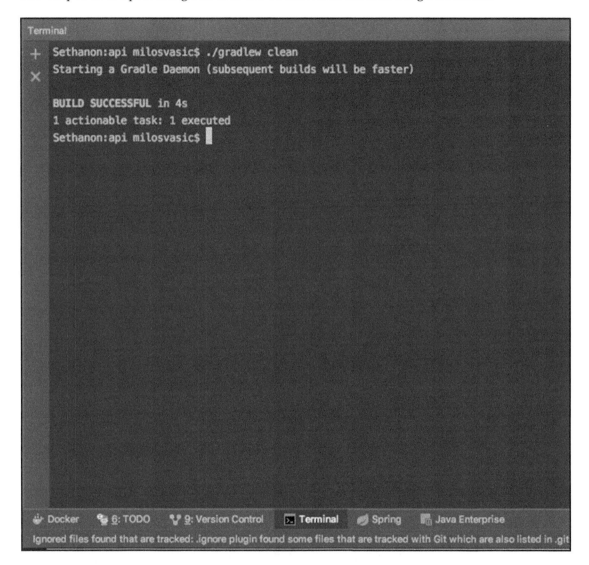

Now, we will perform `./gradlew assemble` to build the application:

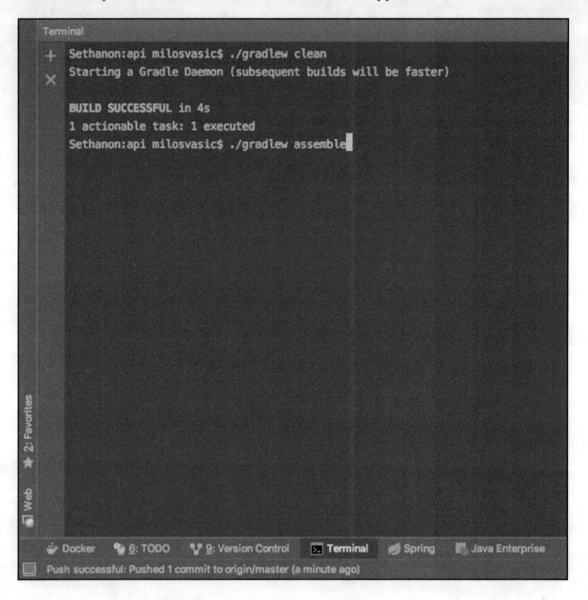

The output of the preceding command is as shown in the following screenshot:

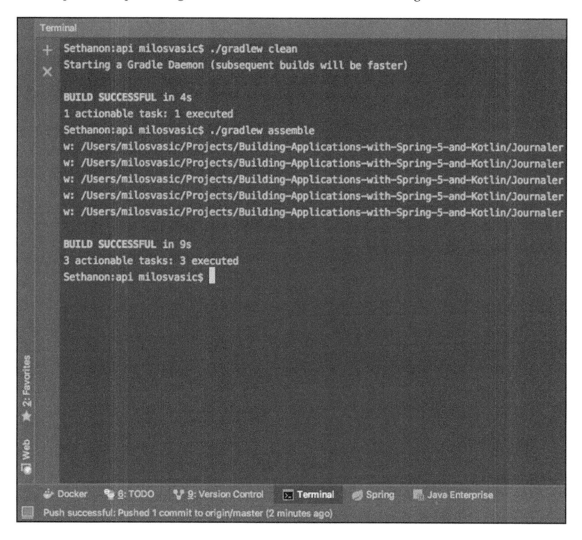

Let's list the content of our project directory by executing the `ls` command:

Navigate to build/libs directory and list the content of the directory using the ls command, as shown in the following screenshot:

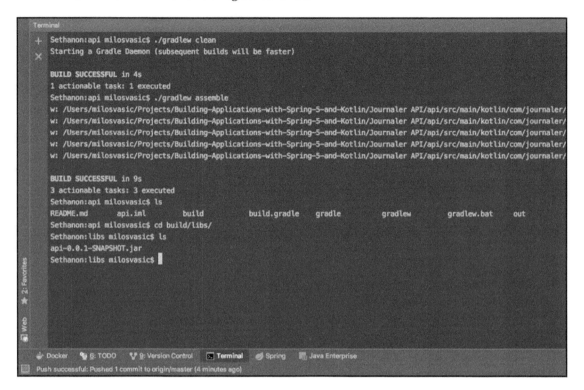

Copy the JAR you see to the location where you want to save it. We will copy it to the `Desktop` for the current user, as shown in the following screenshot:

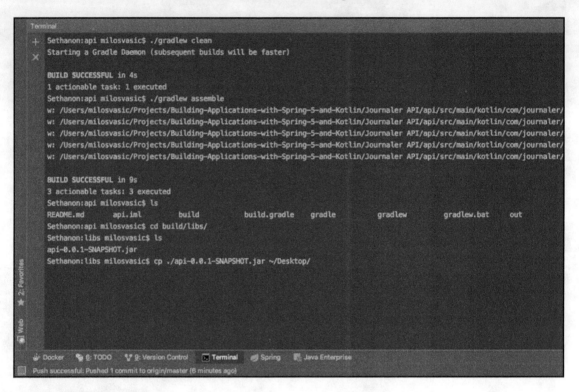

Now, navigate to the location where you just copied the JAR file and try to run it as shown in the following screenshot:

As you can see in the following screenshot, this will fail:

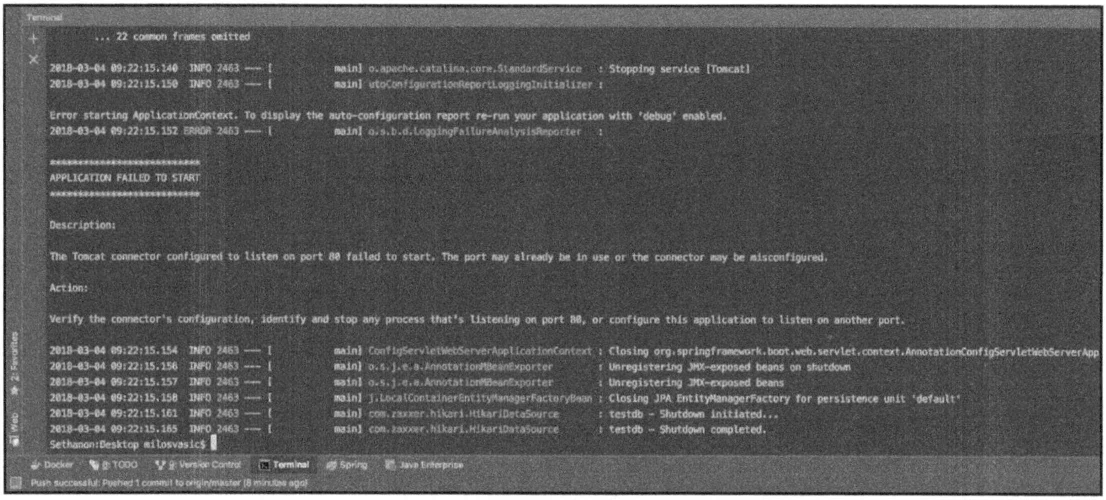

To be able to run our application on port 80, you must run it as a `sudo` user, as shown in the following screenshot:

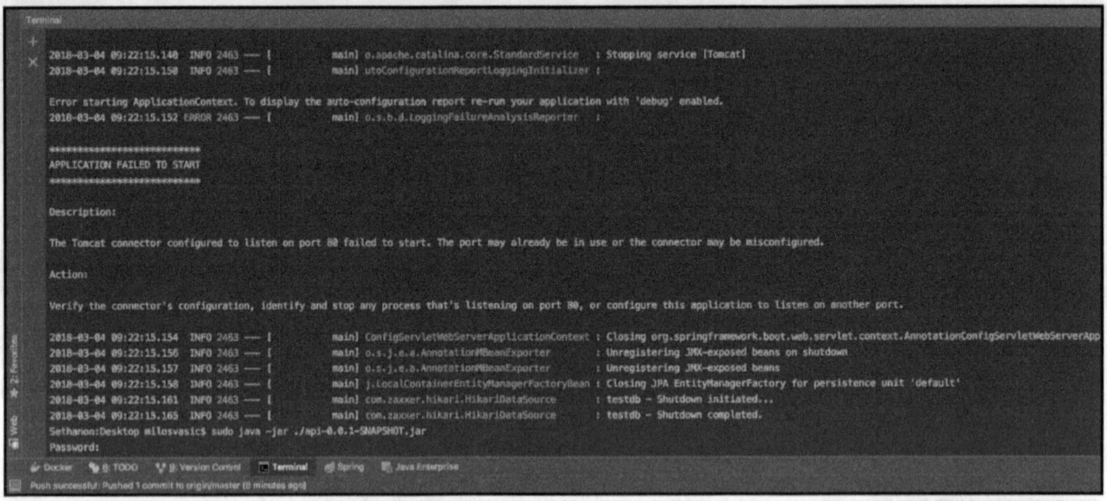

You will be asked for your user's password. Type it in and hit *Enter*. The application will run, as shown in the following screenshot:

Once again, confirm that everything works properly. Open Postman and trigger a couple of API calls, targeting the local host on port 80.

We will insert some notes here:

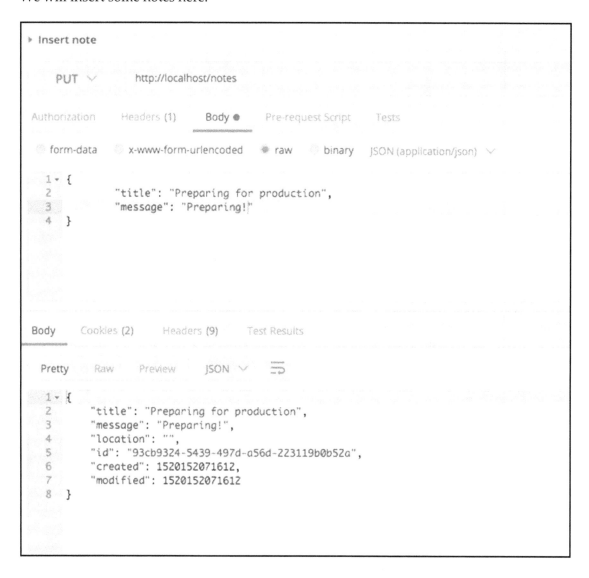

And we will read them:

Once we are sure that this build is fine, we can proceed to the next step in our deployment mission.

Deployment options

In this section, we will explain which options we have regarding Spring application deployment. As you already know, we are using Spring Boot in this project, and this means that Spring Boot provides a public static void main entry point that launches an embedded web server for you.

The `assemble` command we recently performed created a fat JAR for us, so all dependencies are included. If we run the application like we did in the previous section by running `$ java - jar api-0.0.1-SNAPSHOT.jar`.

We will also start the embedded server, and our application will start listening on the port defined in the `application.properties` file.

Deploying the Tomcat application server

By running our JAR, Spring Boot will detect that you have Spring MVC controller and will start up an embedded Apache Tomcat instance. This is its default behavior.

Once the server is running, you will be able to access your application, like we did use Postman in the previous section.

To customize Tomcat, we can use our `application.properties` file and assign miscellaneous configurations, for example:

- `server.tomcat.accept-count=0`: The maximum queue length for incoming connection requests when all possible request processing threads are in use.
- `server.tomcat.accesslog.buffered=true`: Used when you want to buffer the output in such way that it's flushed only periodically.
- `server.tomcat.accesslog.directory=logs`: The directory in which log files are created. This can be absolute or relative to the Tomcat base directory.
- `server.tomcat.accesslog.enabled=false`: Enables the access log.
- `server.tomcat.accesslog.file-date-format=.yyyy-MM-dd`: The date format to place in the log file name.
- `server.tomcat.accesslog.pattern=common`: Format pattern for access logs
- `server.tomcat.accesslog.prefix=access_log`: Log file name prefix.
- `server.tomcat.accesslog.rename-on-rotate=false`: Used when you want to defer the inclusion of the date stamp in the file name until rotate time.

- `server.tomcat.accesslog.request-attributes-enabled=false`: Sets request attributes for the IP address, hostname, protocol, and port used for the request.
- `server.tomcat.accesslog.rotate=true`: Used when you want to enable access log rotation.
- `server.tomcat.accesslog.suffix=.log`: Log file name suffix.
- `server.tomcat.additional-tld-skip-patterns=`: Comma-separated list of additional patterns that match JARs which you wish to ignore for TLD scanning.
- `server.tomcat.background-processor-delay=30s`: Initiates a delay between the invocation of `backgroundProcess` methods (if a duration suffix is not specified, seconds will be used).
- `server.tomcat.basedir=`: The Tomcat base directory. If not specified, a temporary directory is used.
- `server.tomcat.internal-proxies=`: A regular expression matching trusted IP addresses.
- `server.tomcat.max-connections=0`: The maximum number of connections that the server accepts and processes at any given time.
- `server.tomcat.max-http-header-size=0`: The maximum size, in bytes, of the HTTP message header.
- `server.tomcat.max-http-post-size=0`: The maximum size, in bytes, of the HTTP post content.
- `server.tomcat.max-threads=0`: The maximum number of worker threads.
- `server.tomcat.min-spare-threads=0`: The minimum number of worker threads.
- `server.tomcat.port-header=X-Forwarded-Port`: The name of the HTTP header used to override the original port value.
- `server.tomcat.protocol-header=`: The header that holds the incoming protocol, usually named `X-Forwarded-Proto`.
- `server.tomcat.protocol-header-https-value=https`: The value of the protocol header indicating whether the incoming request uses SSL.
- `server.tomcat.redirect-context-root=`: Used to decide whether requests to the context root should be redirected by the appending path or to the path.

- `server.tomcat.remote-ip-header=`: The name of the HTTP header from which the remote IP is extracted, for instance, `X-FORWARDED-FOR`.
- `server.tomcat.resource.cache-ttl=`: The time-to-live of the static resource cache.
- `server.tomcat.uri-encoding=UTF-8`: The character encoding used to decode the URI.
- `server.tomcat.use-relative-redirects=`: Used to decide whether HTTP 1.1 and later location headers generated by a call to `sendRedirect` will use relative or absolute redirects.

The following configurations are specific to the Tomcat data source:

```
spring.datasource.tomcat.*= ...
```

In our application, data source configuration looks like this:

```
spring.datasource.tomcat.test-on-borrow=true
spring.datasource.tomcat.validation-interval=30000
spring.datasource.tomcat.validation-query=SELECT 1
spring.datasource.tomcat.remove-abandoned=true
spring.datasource.tomcat.remove-abandoned-timeout=10000
spring.datasource.tomcat.log-abandoned=true
spring.datasource.tomcat.max-age=1800000
spring.datasource.tomcat.log-validation-errors=true
spring.datasource.tomcat.max-active=50
spring.datasource.tomcat.max-idle=10
```

Deploying to the Java EE application server

To deploy your Spring application to one of the mainstream Java EE application servers, you will need to make a couple of changes in your code, and then your project will be ready. We need a WAR build instead of the JAR for this.

Open `build.gradle` and update it so that the Gradle WAR plugin is applied:

```
buildscript {
    ext {
        kotlinVersion = '1.2.21'
        springBootVersion = '2.0.0.M4'
    }
    repositories {
        mavenCentral()
        maven { url "https://repo.spring.io/snapshot" }
```

```
            maven { url "https://repo.spring.io/milestone" }
    }
    dependencies {
        classpath("org.springframework.boot:spring-boot-gradle-
plugin:${springBootVersion}")
        classpath("org.jetbrains.kotlin:kotlin-gradle-
plugin:${kotlinVersion}")
        classpath("org.jetbrains.kotlin:kotlin-allopen:${kotlinVersion}")
    }
}

apply plugin: 'kotlin'
apply plugin: 'kotlin-spring'
apply plugin: 'eclipse'
apply plugin: 'org.springframework.boot'
apply plugin: 'io.spring.dependency-management'
apply plugin: 'war'

group = 'com.journaler'
version = '0.0.1-SNAPSHOT'
sourceCompatibility = 1.8

compileKotlin {
    kotlinOptions.jvmTarget = "1.8"
}
compileTestKotlin {
    kotlinOptions.jvmTarget = "1.8"
}

repositories {
    mavenCentral()
    maven { url "https://repo.spring.io/snapshot" }
    maven { url "https://repo.spring.io/milestone" }
}

dependencies {
    compile 'org.springframework.boot:spring-boot-starter-security'
    compile 'org.springframework:spring-context'
    compile 'org.springframework:spring-aop'
    compile 'org.springframework.boot:spring-boot-starter'
    compile 'org.springframework.boot:spring-boot-starter-web'
    compile 'org.springframework.boot:spring-boot-starter-actuator'
    compile 'org.springframework:spring-web'
```

```
compile 'org.springframework:spring-webmvc'
runtime 'mysql:mysql-connector-java'
compile 'org.springframework.boot:spring-boot-starter-data-jpa'
compile "org.jetbrains.kotlin:kotlin-stdlib-jdk8:${kotlinVersion}"
compile "org.jetbrains.kotlin:kotlin-reflect:${kotlinVersion}"
testCompile 'org.springframework.boot:spring-boot-starter-test'
providedRuntime 'org.springframework.boot:spring-boot-starter-tomcat'
}
```

Since we use Gradle, the following code marks our servlet container as being provided:

```
providedRuntime 'org.springframework.boot:spring-boot-starter-tomcat'
```

Another modification is required. We must change our ApiApplication class:

```
package com.journaler.api

import org.springframework.boot.SpringApplication
import org.springframework.boot.autoconfigure.SpringBootApplication
import
org.springframework.boot.web.servlet.support.SpringBootServletInitializer
import org.springframework.boot.builder.SpringApplicationBuilder

@SpringBootApplication
class ApiApplication : SpringBootServletInitializer() {
    override fun configure(application: SpringApplicationBuilder):
SpringApplicationBuilder {
        return application.sources(ApiApplication::class.java)
    }
}

fun main(args: Array<String>) {
    SpringApplication.run(ApiApplication::class.java, *args)
}
```

Now, we are ready to generate WAR. Open the Terminal and use Gradle's `./gradlew clean` command, as shown in the following screenshot:

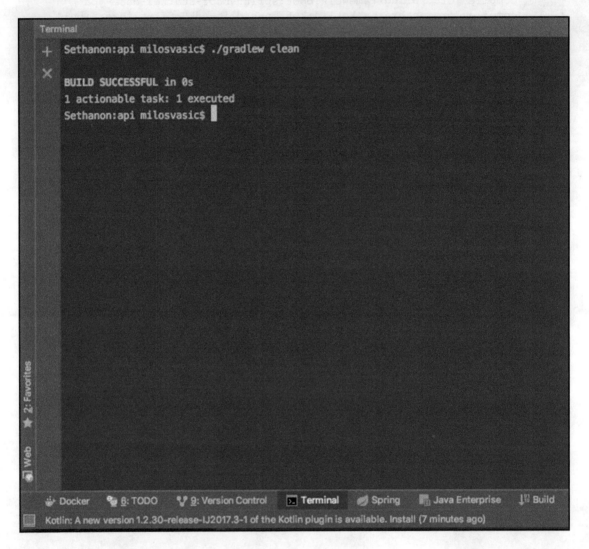

When the preceding command completes its process, run Gradle's `.gradlew assemble` command, as shown in the following screenshot:

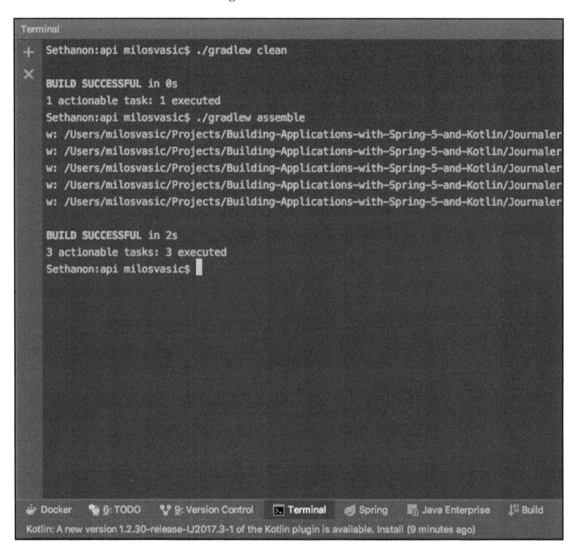

After the preceding command completes its process, we should have our WAR ready. Navigate to the `libs` directory, as shown in the following screenshot:

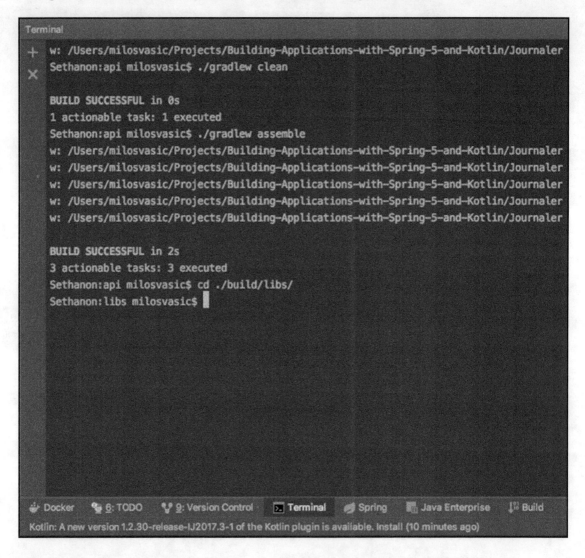

Now, list the files in the directory using the `ls` command, as shown in the following screenshot:

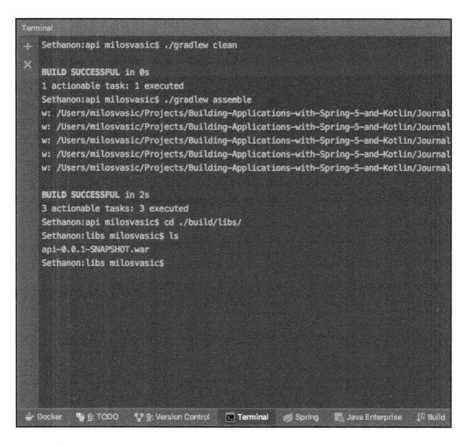

As you can see, the `api-0.0.1-SNAPSHOT.war` build is available.

Deploying to the Cloud (AWS)

Today, **Amazon Web Services** (**AWS**) is the most popular platforms for hosting applications. AWS is a subsidiary of Amazon.com that provides on-demand cloud computing platforms to individuals, companies, and governments, on a paid subscription basis. The reason for its popularity is that it offers reliable, scalable, and inexpensive cloud computing services.

Since this is the last section of this chapter, we will guide you through the process of deploying to AWS step by step. We will show you how to deploy our API Spring Boot application using AWS Elastic Beanstalk. We will also show you how to customize the Spring Boot configuration through the use of environment variables.

AWS Elastic Beanstalk provides convention over configuration, but it still gives us the ability to make adjustments if needed. Elastic Beanstalk is a managed service designed for deploying and scaling web applications and services. It supports various programming languages, as well as a variety of web and application servers, for example, Apache, Nginx, Passenger, Tomcat, and IIS.

To be able to deploy our application, we need to set up an AWS account. You can sign up for a free account to try out AWS Elastic Beanstalk here: `https://aws.amazon.com/free/`.

Open the link. You should see the following AWS Free Tier page:

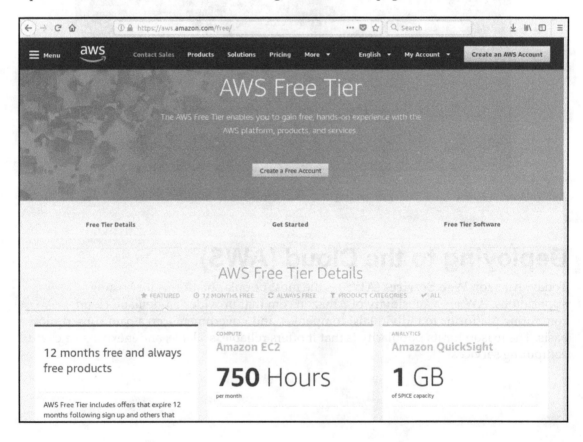

Click on the **Create a Free Account** button. The registration form will appear:

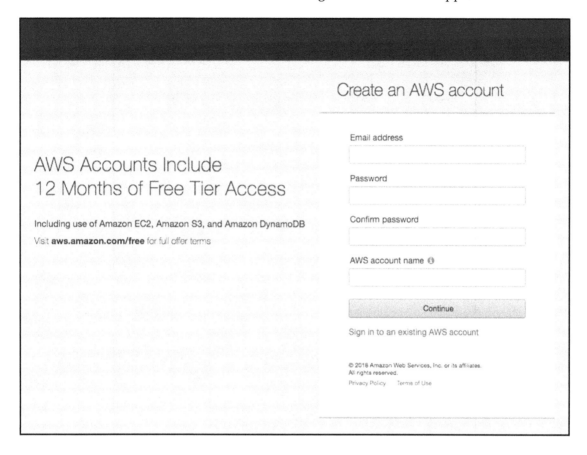

Populate your data and click on **Continue**. Then, the **Contact Information** form will appear:

Insert your personal data and click on the **Create Account and Continue** button. Then, the following **Payment Information** form will appear:

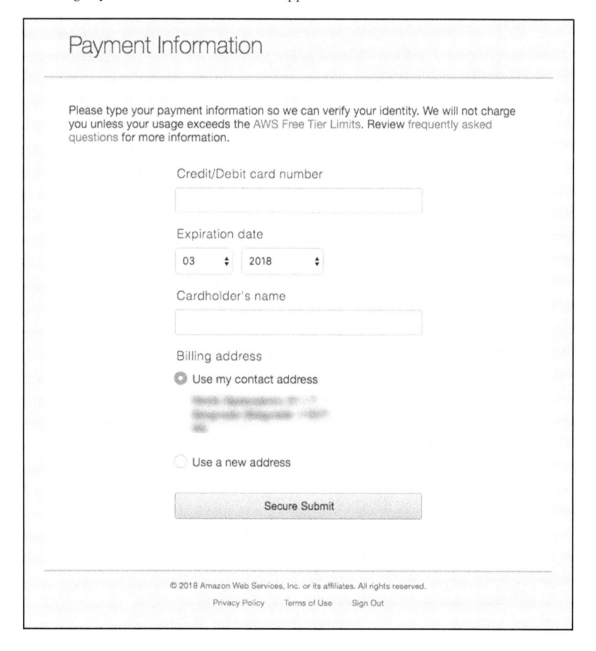

As it says on the AWS website: **Please type in your payment information so that we can verify your identity. We will not charge you unless your usage exceeds the AWS Free Tier limits.**

Populate your data and click on the **Secure Submit** button to continue. Then, the following **Phone Verification** page will appear:

Follow the **Phone Verification** instructions until the verification process is completed:

Click **Continue** and choose the **Basic Plan** by clicking on the **Free** button:

Select a Support Plan

AWS offers a selection of support plans to meet your needs. Choose the support plan that best aligns with your AWS usage. Learn more

Basic Plan	**Developer Plan**	**Business Plan**
Free	From $29/month	From $100/month

Basic Plan

- Included with all accounts
- 24/7 self-service access to forums and resources
- Best practice checks to help improve security and performance
- Access to health status and notifications

Developer Plan

- For early adoption, testing and development
- Email access to AWS Support during business hours
- 1 primary contact can open an unlimited number of support cases
- 12-hour response time for nonproduction systems

Business Plan

- For production workloads & business-critical dependencies
- 24/7 chat, phone, and email access to AWS Support
- Unlimited contacts can open an unlimited number of support cases
- 1-hour response time for production systems

Need Enterprise level support?

Contact your account manager for additional information on running business and mission critical-workloads on AWS (starting at $15,000/month). Learn more

Congratulations! You have successfully registered for an AWS account:

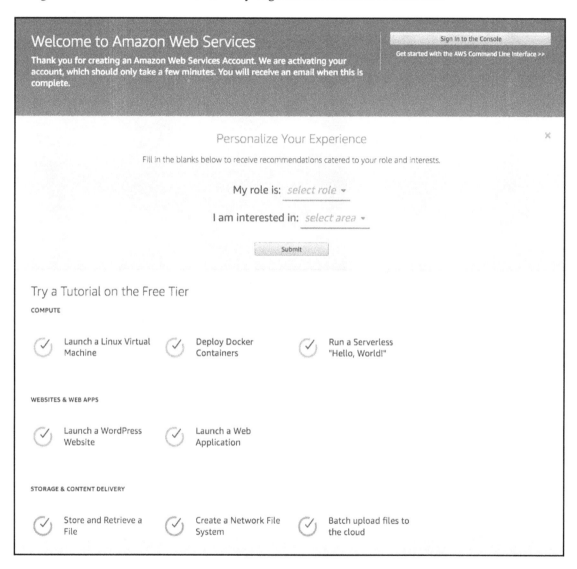

Now, click on the **Sign in to the Console** button on the top right-hand side. The **Sign in** form will appear:

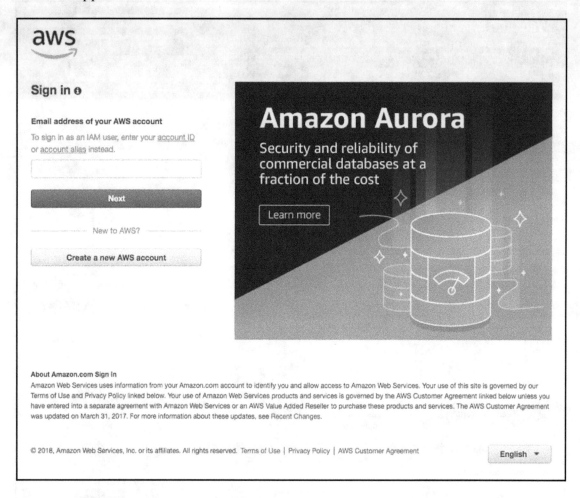

Fill this in with your information and click on the **Next** button to continue. Fill in the password and continue forward. After a couple of seconds, you will be redirected to the AWS Management Console:

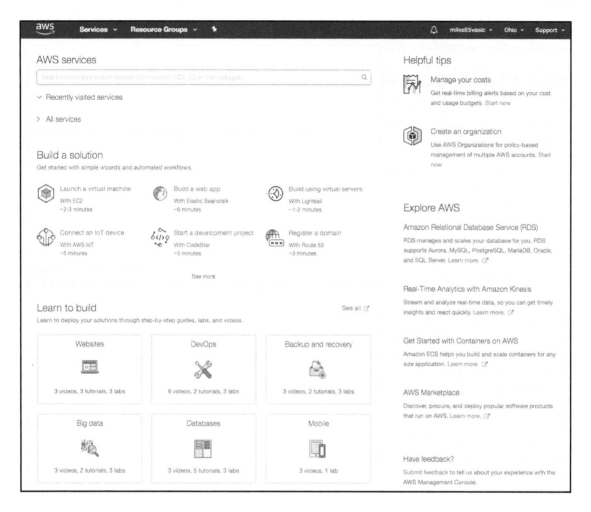

Now, we are ready to deploy our application!

By the time you read this book, the Amazon AWS registration procedure and registration flow may have changed. In that case, we encourage you to simply follow the registration steps since it's easy to register and understand each step.

Open the **Elastic Beanstalk** console by clicking on the **Build a web app** link. The **Elastic Beanstalk console** will open:

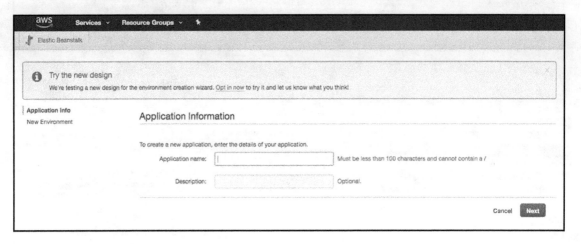

For the **Application name**, enter Journaler API, and for the **Description**, enter Example application. Click on the **Next** button. A page called **New Environment** will appear:

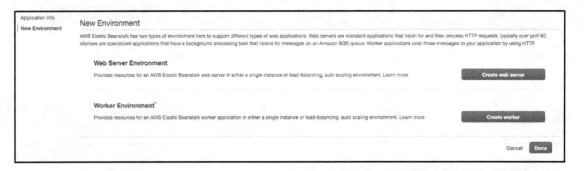

Click on the **Create web server** button. A page called **Environment Type** will appear:

For the **Predefined configuration**, choose **Java**. For the **Environment type**, choose **Single instance**. Click on the **Next** button to continue. A page called **Application Version** will appear:

Choose **Upload your own** and the click on the **Choose File** button. Navigate to the location where you saved your JAR and select it:

Click on the **Next** button to upload the JAR:

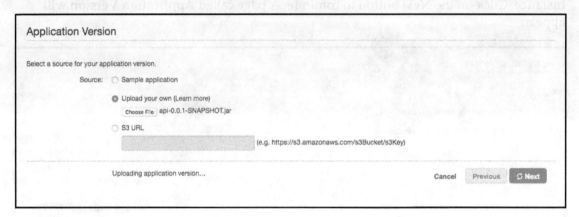

It will take some time to upload this version of our application. The following **Environment Information** page will appear:

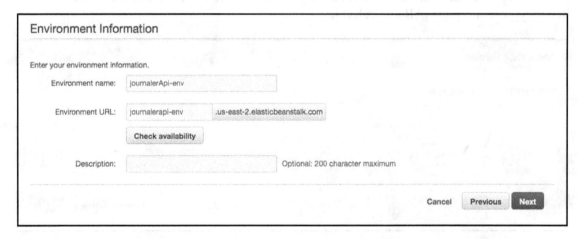

Click on the **Check availability** button before continuing. After the check is completed, our API URL will become green:

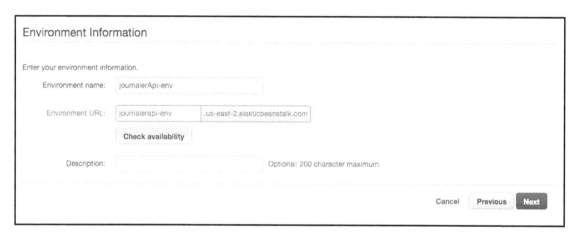

Write down the full URL for your application. In our case, that would be the following:

```
journalerapi-env.us-east-2.elasticbeanstalk.com
```

Now, click on the **Next** button. The following **Additional Resources** page will appear:

Check both checkboxes and click on the **Next** button. Populate the following **Configuration Details** page:

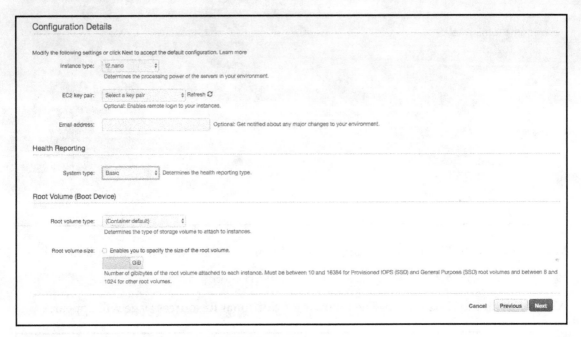

Click on the **Next** button to continue. The following **Environment Tags** page will appear:

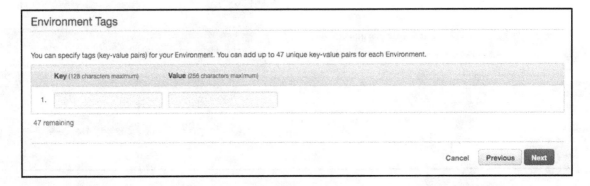

Click on the **Next** button to continue. The following **RDS Configuration** page will appear:

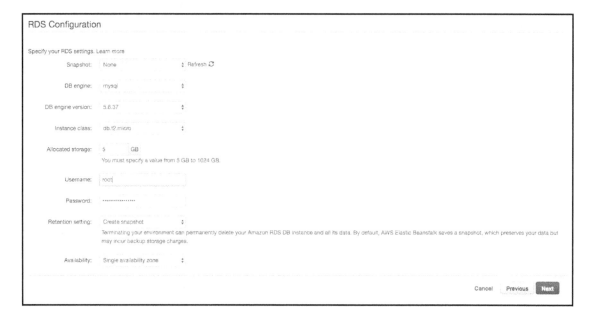

For the username and password, put in the values we used in our
`application.properties` file. Fill in the form with this data and click on the **Next** button
to continue. The following **VPC Configuration** page will appear:

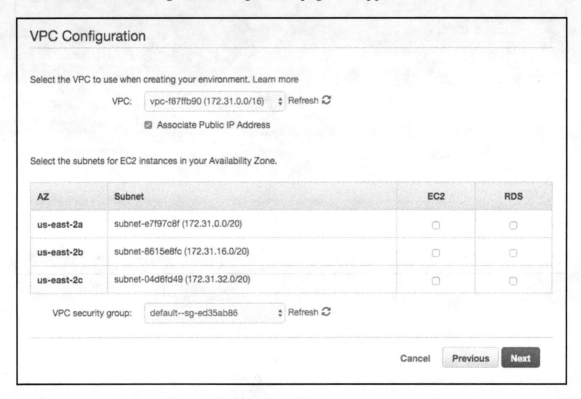

Select **Associate Public IP Address**:

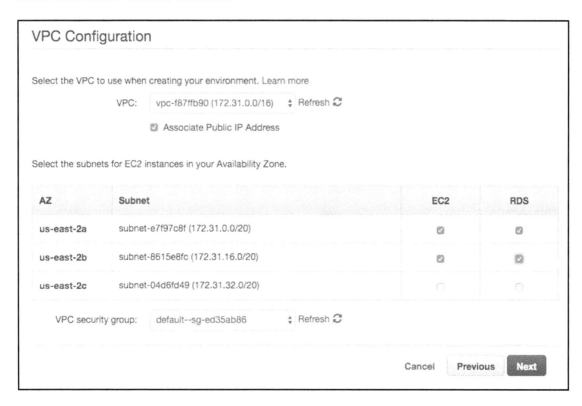

When done, click on the **Next** button to continue. The following **Permissions** page will appear:

Click on the **Next** button. The following **Review** page will appear:

Application Info	**Review**
New Environment	
Environment Type	Review the following information. Then click "Launch."
Application Version	
Environment Info	**Application Info**
Additional Resources	
Configuration Details	**Application name** Journaler API
Environment Tags	**Description** Example application.
RDS Configuration	
VPC Configuration	**New Environment**
Permissions	
Review Information	**Tier** Web Server

Environment Type

Container type 64bit Amazon Linux 2017.09 v2.6.6 running Java 8

Environment type Single instance

Application Version

Application source C:\fakepath\api-0.0.1-SNAPSHOT.jar

Environment Info

Environment name journalerApi-env

Environment URL http://journalerapi-env.us-east-2.elasticbeanstalk.com

Configuration Details

Instance type t2.nano

Key pair

Email address (default)

Root volume type (default)

Root volume size (default)

Root volume IOPS

Review the configurations and click **Launch** to finish the wizard. The deployment will begin:

It will take some time to complete the deployment. Wait until the deployment completes:

Congratulations! You deployed your application successfully! Before we try it out, there are a few more things left to do.

By default, our Spring Boot application will listen on port 80. Elastic Beanstalk assumes that the application will listen on port 5000. We must fix this.

On the **Configuration** page in your environment, locate **Software Configuration**:

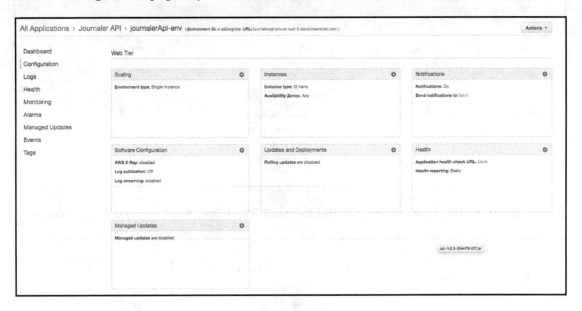

Observe the Software Configuration option in the Configuration page

Click the settings icon and scroll to the bottom of the page:

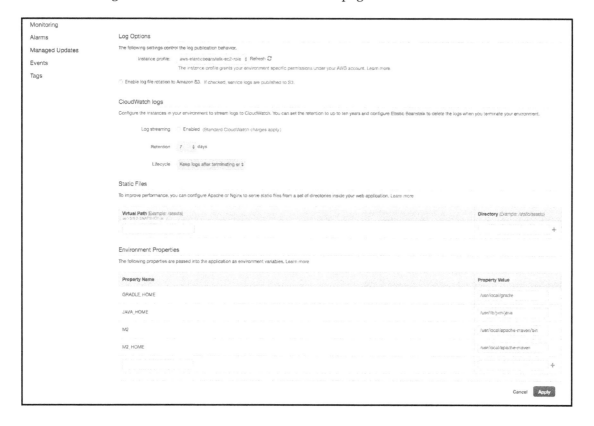

Add a **SERVER_PORT** value of 5000:

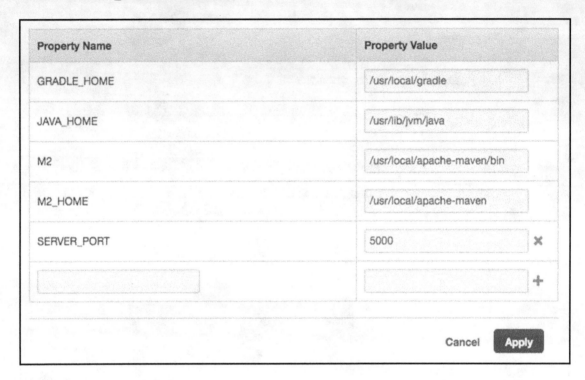

Property Name	Property Value
GRADLE_HOME	/usr/local/gradle
JAVA_HOME	/usr/lib/jvm/java
M2	/usr/local/apache-maven/bin
M2_HOME	/usr/local/apache-maven
SERVER_PORT	5000

Cancel **Apply**

Click on the **Apply** button to save changes. In addition to configuring the port the application listens on, we must also specify the environment variables to configure the database that the application will be using.

Let's obtain the database's endpoint URL. On the **Environment Configuration** page, under the **Data Tier** section, you'll find the endpoint under **RDS**:

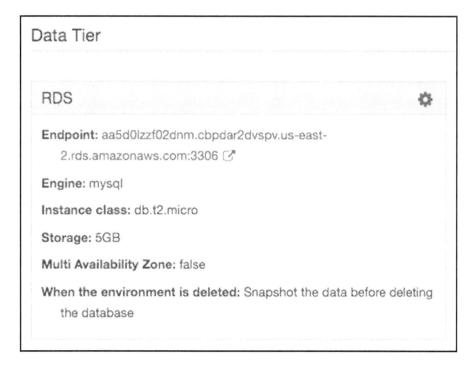

Write it down. In our case, it's as follows:

```
aa5d0lzzf02dnm.cbpdar2dvspv.us-east-2.rds.amazonaws.com:3306
```

Go back to the **Environment Properties** section and extend it with the following:

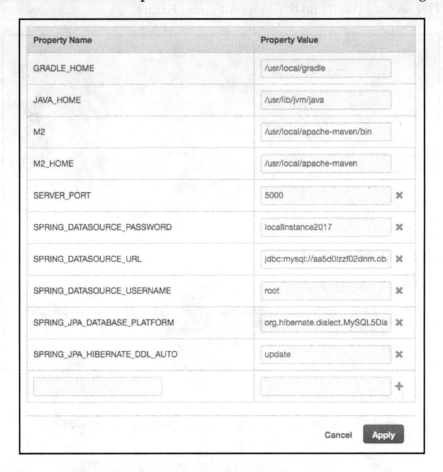

To summarize, we added the following environment properties:

- **SERVER_PORT**: 5000
- **SPRING_DATASOURCE_PASSWORD**: localInstance2017
- **SPRING_DATASOURCE_URL**: jdbc:mysql://aa5d0lzzf02dnm.cbpdar2dv
  spv.us-east-2.rds.amazonaws.com:3306/ebdb (you will use your DB URL)

Pay attention! The URL ends with: /ebdb

- **SPRING_DATASOURCE_USERNAME:** root
- **SPRING_JPA_DATABASE_PLATFORM:**
  org.hibernate.dialect.MySQL5Dialect
- **SPRING_JPA_HIBERNATE_DDL_AUTO:** update

Click on **Apply** to save changes and wait until the changes are applied. Now, you are ready to try out the API. Open Postman and execute a couple of API calls targeting our API's production URL.

It can take some time for the application to be ready! Refresh the application's URL until error 502 stops appearing. You will know that the application is ready when you see Spring's **Whitelabel Error Page**:

Let's insert some notes. We will replace our localhost URL with our production one (put in the URL you wrote down during deployment):

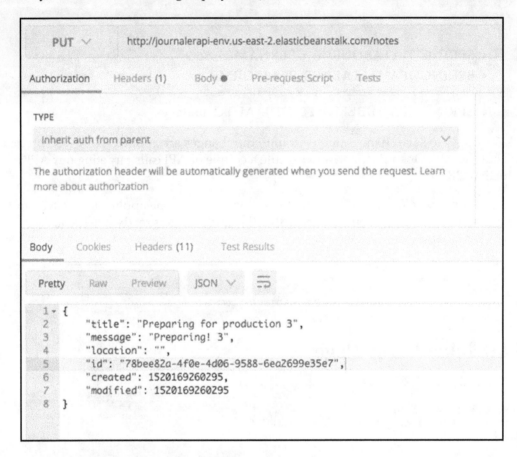

Once you have inserted the notes, verify that they are really there:

```
    GET  ∨        http://journalerapi-env.us-east-2.elasticbeanstalk.com/notes

Authorization    Headers           Pre-request Script    Tests

TYPE

  Inherit auth from parent                                              ∨

The authorization header will be automatically generated when you send the request. Learn
more about authorization


Body    Cookies    Headers (11)    Test Results

Pretty    Raw    Preview    JSON  ∨   ⇥

  1 ▾ [
  2 ▾     {
  3             "title": "Preparing for production 3",
  4             "message": "Preparing! 3",
  5             "location": "",
  6             "id": "92638a45-6623-44e6-b02d-5f6e88b5a927",
  7             "created": 1520169252000,
  8             "modified": 1520169252000
  9         },
 10 ▾     {
 11             "title": "Preparing for production 3",
 12             "message": "Preparing! 3",
 13             "location": "",
 14             "id": "9eb85473-878a-4e9f-bb1d-867f723e702a",
 15             "created": 1520169258000,
 16             "modified": 1520169258000
 17         },
 18 ▾     {
 19             "title": "Preparing for production 3",
 20             "message": "Preparing! 3",
 21             "location": "",
 22             "id": "048215d9-2b79-4fb0-985a-a2608f5a2c98",
 23             "created": 1520169260000,
 24             "modified": 1520169260000
 25         },
 26 ▾     {
 27             "title": "Preparing for production 3",
 28             "message": "Preparing! 3",
 29             "location": "",
 30             "id": "78bee82a-4f0e-4d06-9588-6ea2699e35e7",
 31             "created": 1520169260000,
 32             "modified": 1520169260000
 33         }
 34 ]
```

Finally, we can confirm that our Rest API is up and running! Now, you can expose it to client applications. You can use it with Angular clients, Android, iOS applications, or any other you choose.

Once you release the new version of the application (when the new JAR is ready), it's very simple to deploy it. All you have to do is use the landing page of the AWS **Elastic Beanstalk** console and upload a new build. All of the environment properties we set will be used and the application will be ready instantly.

It's up to you to decide which method for deployment you will use. Investigate and compare other options. Write down all of the pros and cons. Try each and every one of them. We recommend AWS as our preferred application deployment method since it's easy to configure and deploy, and it's stable and flexible.

Summary

In this chapter, we released our application to production. This was a perfect way to finish our journey through this book. During the chapters of this book, we sculptured the application and, in the grand finale, we deployed it to AWS. Spring is a big framework and it can take some time to learn everything it has to offer. We encourage you to keep learning and improving your Spring knowledge. Write as much code as you can and investigate all of the options Spring gives to you. As we already mentioned at the end of the previous section, try all of the deployment options you can. Knowing each of them can be a huge advantage!

For further reading, we recommend you look at the official Spring documentation or books that target specific Spring-related areas. Don't hesitate and get into the action. Create a new repository and start writing your new Spring application!

Other Books You May Enjoy

If you enjoyed this book, you may be interested in these other books by Packt:

Reactive Programming in Kotlin
Rivu Chakraborty

ISBN: 978-1-78847-302-6

- Learn about reactive programming paradigms and how reactive programming can improve your existing projects
- Gain in-depth knowledge in RxKotlin 2.0 and the ReactiveX Framework
- Use RxKotlin with Android
- Create your own custom operators in RxKotlin
- Use Spring Framework 5.0 with Kotlin
- Use the reactor-kotlin extension
- Build Rest APIs with Spring, Hibernate, and RxKotlin
- Use test subscriber to test RxKotlin applications
- Use backpressure management and Flowables

Learning Spring Boot 2.0 - Second Edition
Greg L. Turnquist

ISBN: 978-1-78646-378-4

- Create powerful, production-grade applications and services with minimal fuss
- Support multiple environments with one artifact, and add production-grade support with features
- Find out how to tweak your apps through different properties
- Use custom metrics to track the number of messages published and consumed
- Enhance the security model of your apps
- Make use of reactive programming in Spring Boot
- Build anything from lightweight unit tests to fully running embedded web container integration tests

Leave a review - let other readers know what you think

Please share your thoughts on this book with others by leaving a review on the site that you bought it from. If you purchased the book from Amazon, please leave us an honest review on this book's Amazon page. This is vital so that other potential readers can see and use your unbiased opinion to make purchasing decisions, we can understand what our customers think about our products, and our authors can see your feedback on the title that they have worked with Packt to create. It will only take a few minutes of your time, but is valuable to other potential customers, our authors, and Packt. Thank you!

Index

www.ingramcontent.com/pod-product-compliance
Lightning Source LLC
Chambersburg PA
CBHW080626060326
40690CB00021B/4825